how to
freeze

how to freeze

everything you need to know
about freezing and
freezer management

Carolyn Humphries

foulsham
LONDON • NEW YORK • TORONTO • SYDNEY

foulsham

The Publishing House, Bennetts Close,
Cippenham, Slough, Berkshire, SL1 5AP

ISBN 0-572-02769-9

Copyright © 2002 W. Foulsham & Co Ltd.

Cover photograph © Anthony Blake Photo Library

Printed in Great Britain by Cox & Wyman Ltd, Reading, Berkshire

contents

introduction

There are lots of books on the subject of freezing, but this one is different. There is no complicated terminology. It tells you exactly what to do and when to do it in an easy-reference format – it's as simple as that!

I haven't wasted space on information on buying a freezer as the chances are you already own one. However, I will offer just two pieces of advice. Get the biggest one you can afford and accommodate – you will always wish you had bought a larger one! Also I would not recommend buying a combined fridge/freezer – if one part breaks down and is irreparable, you don't want to have to ditch the whole thing, so buy them as two separate units.

Freezer management is crucial, and I offer a foolproof system. Without labels, every piece of frozen food tends to end up looking the same and then it's all too easy to thaw stewing beef, thinking it's lean, tender rump or to tip frozen crushed strawberries into your Bolognese sauce, thinking they are tomatoes from the previous year!

The second part of this book gives you straightforward information on the preparation and packaging of foods to be frozen. If food is just popped into the freezer, willy-nilly, without any preparation, then it will most certainly spoil, tasting tough and unpleasant on thawing. Packing is important too. Food won't keep in peak condition if you leave it in thin plastic bags from the supermarket; in fact, it will spoil very quickly.

All the methods in this book are simple and it's packed with all the basic information you need for successful freezing. You can see exactly what you can and can't freeze, how to do it, and for how long it can be stored. There are tips on batch baking, defrosting and cooking from frozen too. In fact, *How to Freeze* tells you everything you need to know about freezing!

freezer management and maintenance

A well-stocked freezer is a great asset, saving you time and trouble. But it can only do this if you know what's in it and how to find it instantly. Rummaging around for ages, looking for the right meat amongst all the anonymous packages is crazy. You will be getting frostbite, while the contents of your freezer warm up and the machine burns extra electricity trying to compensate for being open for so long. It need never happen as long as you use a system of labelling.

Labelling

Many so-called experts recommend keeping a book, in which you list the contents of each package and when you freeze it (so you'll know when it should be eaten by). Others swear by colour coding. Sadly, in my experience, even the best of us can only keep methods like this up for a week or two, then it's just too much hassle looking for the book, or we don't have the right coloured pen and we're back to that mountain of UFOs – unidentified frozen objects. But, be warned: if you don't have some way of telling what's what, even if you're convinced you'll remember what each item is, I guarantee that a month later you won't have a clue!

No-effort marking

The solution, I have discovered, is my system of No-effort Marking. The only vital tools are a marker pen and white sticky labels.

1 Simply write on the left-hand side of the label what the food is, the date and the quantity.

2 Then on the right, mark a large, bold letter (as big as you can get on the label) depicting what sort of food it is. Also, if you have time and space, add any tips of extra flavouring or thickening needed when defrosted.

3 Stick it on the bag or container.

The choice of letters you use is up to you. For example:

* M – meat and poultry
* F – fish
* V – vegetables
* Fr – fruit
* C – cakes
* B – bread
* P – pastry
* S – sauces
* So – soups
* D – dessert

The letters are self-explanatory but to be on the safe side, keep a list of them written on the inside of the freezer door, or stuck to the front. Also, if possible, keep different foods on different shelves or in different baskets for easier finding – fruit and veg in one area, meat and fish in another, bread and cakes in a third, sauces, soups and 'bits and pieces' in another. Of course, this lovely system does tend to go out of the window when you come home from the supermarket with a load of bargains to be frozen immediately and have space only on one shelf or in one basket! But as long as you use the labelling system and the large letter is easy to see, you should never have a problem. Try and get in the habit of rearranging everything properly as soon as a space becomes available. But don't get obsessive about it!

Colour coding

Colour coding can be used in much the same way, instead of the system of letters. One of the simplest ways is to use different coloured sticky freezer labels. Using an indelible pen, write what the food is, the quantity, the date and any special instructions on the labels as before and stick them on polythene bags or rigid containers.

You could use colours like this:

* Red – meat
* Green – vegetables
* Blue – fish
* Yellow – fruit
* White – baked good, such as bread, pastry (paste), etc., plus sweet dishes made with chocolate, coffee and so on that don't fall into any of the other categories

Again, you must make sure you write your code on the inside of the freezer door (or stick it to the front) so that you remember it and other members of the family understand it when they are rummaging around.

An alternative to the coloured labels is to use plain labels but with different coloured indelible pens, chinagraph or waxed pencils (if using this method use a black marker for baked goods as white won't show up). You can also use appropriately coloured twist ties for bags, or you can buy different coloured freezer tapes to seal bags and stick on to rigid containers.

A third way is to buy very large different coloured plastic bags. You then put all your meat in the red one, veg in the green one and so on. The only thing you MUST remember is to put them in the right bags. But even if you don't do it all the time, at least some of your foods will be quickly identifiable!

You can also use small coloured plastic bags and rigid containers with different coloured lids to match your code, but they are more expensive than ordinary freezer bags and containers. There is also the danger that you will run out of the colour you want to use. Then you'll end up putting the food in the wrong coloured bag or box and the system will be ruined. So perhaps it's best to stick to my No-effort Marking.

Food rotation

It is important that you don't keep putting new foods on the top of older items, otherwise you will simply keep using the freshest food, leaving the rest to fester underneath. In the supermarket, you will have seen the assistants pulling the older packs to the front, putting the fresher goods behind them, and you should do the same. Try to use up one whole batch of meat, for instance, before starting on the new one, and eat the apple turnovers you made two months ago in preference to the little apple pies you made only last week.

Manageable quantities

When you're unpacking your shopping, instead of pushing the food quickly into the freezer, stop and think for a second. If, for instance, you've bought a family pack of 12 pork chops at a bargain price, are you going to eat them all at once? Probably not – so separate them into the numbers you are likely to use in one go, wrap them properly (see Wrapping food, page 14), and label them before putting into the freezer. In the same way, if you have a glut of fruit or your runner beans from the garden all crop at once, always freeze them in usable quantities (say, enough for two or four servings) so you never have to thaw more than you need.

Storage times

Don't make the mistake of thinking that food lasts in the freezer indefinitely. Although a mammoth discovered under the ice has been preserved for thousands of years, anything frozen does deteriorate after a while and some items more quickly than others. So do take note of the recommended storage times throughout the book and endeavour to eat the foods within that period. It won't do you any harm to eat them later, but the texture and flavour will become impaired, so you may not enjoy them very much.

Cleaning your freezer

It is important to keep the freezer clean and hygienic.

* Before you use your new freezer for the first time, wipe it out with a clean cloth rinsed in a bowl of hot water with 15 ml/1 tbsp bicarbonate of soda (baking soda) added. You should do this every time you defrost it too.
* Wipe the outer surfaces regularly with a clean, damp cloth, rinsed in detergent or an anti-bacterial cleaner, and clean around the seals.
* Make sure you remove any spills or damaged bags of food as soon as you notice them.
* If your freezer is stored in a garage or outhouse, polish the outside with silicone wax from time to time to protect it.
* Brush the dust and cobwebs off the pipes and wires at the back of the freezer from time to time if possible – if it's built-in this will only be possible when it is serviced, however.

Most manufacturers recommend that a recognised engineer services your freezer once a year.

Defrosting your freezer

Some freezers are self-defrosting but if not, you will need to defrost the freezer at least once a year for a chest freezer and two or three times a year for an upright model. In between times, scrape off any frosty ice that accumulates inside with a plastic scraper (usually provided with your freezer).

It's best to defrost your freezer when your stocks are low. It is a good idea either to deliberately run down the amount of food so you can do this or to choose a time of year when it is naturally less full – perhaps before you go fruit picking in the summer, before your garden produce is in full flourish or before you have a massive stock-up for Christmas.

* Ideally choose a cool day.
* You will need to insulate the food so that it does not defrost while it is out of the freezer. Place an old blanket or layers of newspapers on the floor and pile the freezer contents on top. Wrap thoroughly, packing any quick-thaw items, such as ice cream, in the middle of the pile, so they are protected by other frozen objects around them.
* Switch off your freezer.
* Lay more newspaper or an old towel around the base to mop up any water that may trickle out.
* Put bowls of hot water on the shelves and the base of the freezer, to speed up the melting process.
* If your freezer has a drain hole, attach the pipe that comes with the freezer to the hole and place a large bowl under it to catch the thawed ice.
* Close the door for a few minutes so that the temperature inside rises with the heat of the water.
* As soon as the ice begins to melt, knock it off with a plastic scraper – NEVER use a metal knife or wire brush or you may damage the machine. Remove in lumps from the cabinet.
* Keep replacing the hot water as it cools.
* When all the ice is gone, wipe out the cabinet with a clean cloth, rinsed in hot water with 15 ml/1 tbsp bicarbonate of soda (baking soda) added. Dry with a dry cloth.
* Set the freezer to 'fast-freeze' and close the cabinet. After 15 minutes check that it is working properly, then sort the food and return it to the freezer. Keep back anything that has reached the end of its storage time and use it immediately.
* Turn the freezer back to 'normal' setting after 2–3 hours.

Insurance

Most manufacturers recommend you take out an extended warranty to protect the freezer and food against accidental damage. Weigh up the cost – you may find it very expensive measured against your potential loss. Also check out your house contents insurance policy; your freezer and its contents may well be covered by this, and if not, it may be a relatively low extra cost to have them included.

In case of breakdown

Many freezers now have warning light or an alarm, which will sound if the freezer temperature rises above $-18°C/0°F$. If yours goes off, don't panic and rush to call an engineer. You may be able to solve the problem yourself.

First, check to see if the control lights on the freezer are lit. If not, there may have been a power cut. Check your cooker or microwave to see if their displays are lit. If they are flashing, the power has gone off but has now come back on. If there is no sign of life, the power is still off. If there has been a power cut, see page 15. If the freezer is definitely off, check the following list.

1 Make sure that the electrical plug has not been accidentally switched off. (It's a good idea to tape over the plug in its socket so this can't happen.)
2 Check the fuse in the plug has not blown.
3 Check the mains: has the trip switch for the whole house been triggered or has the fuse for the circuit supplying the freezer blown?

If the freezer appears to be on, check this list.

1 Cast your mind back: if you have put too much unfrozen food in the freezer at one go, this will raise the temperature, as will rummaging around too much, keeping the lid or door open for too long.
2 Check that nothing is preventing the lid or door shutting properly.
3 Check that the seals are not damaged.
4 Make sure that the ice has not built up too much inside – this will prevent the machine from working efficiently.
5 Think about the weather – is it exceptionally hot outside and have you have been opening the freezer a lot?
6 Check that air can circulate round the outside of the cabinet (it should not be placed directly against a wall – check your instruction booklet for details).
7 Clean off any grime that may be clogging the condenser and pipes.

If you still can't solve the problem, call an engineer.

What about the contents?

Resist the temptation to open the freezer. The contents will keep perfectly well for up to 24 hours before starting to defrost. The fuller the freezer, the more time you have.

If you have been away and you have no idea how long the freezer has not been working, you may still be able to salvage some of the contents. Check every item, as follows:

* If there are still ice crystals inside the item and it feels very cold, all items can be re-frozen.
* If there are no ice crystals but the food still feels cold, fruit and baked goods, such as bread, cakes, etc., can be re-frozen.

  Raw meat, fish and poultry in this condition cannot be re-frozen. However, they can be cooked and then re-frozen.

  Vegetables like this should be cooked and eaten, or made into soup or other made-up dishes then re-frozen for no longer than 3 months.

  Cooked dishes should be reheated and eaten. Do not re-freeze.

Power cuts

If you suspect there has been a power cut, look at an electric clock or your central heating timer. It will tell you how long the power has been off. If the power is still off, phone the emergency line of your electricity supplier and find out how long the cut is going to last.

Don't open the freezer. If it is full, it will stay frozen for at least 24 hours, half-full, about 12 hours. Most power cuts will be rectified long before this.

As a damage prevention precaution (which probably won't be needed), pack newspapers or old towels round the base of the freezer to mop up any water if the contents start to thaw out completely.

If the power doesn't come back on in plenty of time, consider asking family, friends or a friendly shopkeeper (not affected by the same cut, of course!) if you can borrow space in their freezer for your food. You will then have to pack it up in insulated bags, or put in boxes, wrapped in plenty of newspapers; blankets or towels to insulate it while you transport it.

If it's too late and the food is defrosting, see the checklist on page 14 for what to do with the contents.

packing and storing

Just as you protect yourself from the cold, so you must protect your food in the freezer – or the equivalent of frostbite will occur and it will lose colour, texture, nutrients and flavour. To prevent oxidation, which makes the food smell and taste unpleasant, all air must be excluded too (see page 20 for how do to this).

Freezer wrapping

There are loads of suitable wrappings and containers available to store your frozen food properly. Here are the most useful.

Clingfilm (plastic wrap)

You must use clingfilm that is suitable for the freezer. I recommend a multi-purpose one, which can be used in the microwave and for other food wrapping too. Check that the film complies with the government recommendations for general food use.

Foil

Heavy-duty foil is best because it won't tear easily. Use it to cover foods as a lid over an open container, to wrap bread, meat, cakes and other solid items completely, and to protect bone ends before wrapping in clingfilm or polythene bags. You can just twist and fold foil to secure it but this must be done tightly or the package will come undone. If necessary, seal with freezer tape (see page 19). Foil is available in various widths and lengths in rolls, or in single sheets. The big advantage is that foods can be thawed and reheated in the foil if appropriate (but not in the microwave of course!).

Foil containers

Rigid foil containers are ideal for storing everything from chunky soups to casseroles. You can also use them both to cook and freeze prepared dishes, which can then be thawed and reheated in the same dish in a conventional oven. They usually come with foil-lined cardboard lids, which can be written on for easy labelling. Foil containers are designed to be disposable but sometimes can be re-used; scrub very thoroughly to avoid contamination.

Foil bags

These are ideal for freezing liquids, such as soups or sauces, as they have a polythene lining and are very strong and leak-proof. (A cheaper alternative is to freeze the liquid in a polythene bag placed in a rigid container; you can then remove the rigid container once the contents are solid. Square or rectangular containers are best for this as they make frozen shapes that are easy to stack and store.)

Heavy-duty polythene bags

These are specially designed for freezing food and come in a variety of sizes, either loose or in rolls. I find it's useful to have a few small ones to hand for those little odds and ends you need to freeze, but on the whole, medium-sized bags, about 20 × 30 cm (8 × 12 in) are most useful for an average family. Experience will tell you what suits your requirements best.

Ordinary plastic bags should not be used – they will split easily, exposing the food to the ice and causing freezer burn (a whitish-grey discoloration of the surface, spoiling its texture and flavour), and, of course, spilled free-flow foods like peas, raspberries and breadcrumbs will spread themselves to every corner of the appliance. That said, in an emergency ordinary bags will do the job, provided they are tied tightly and overwrapped completely with foil.

Rigid containers

Made of polythene or other hard plastic, with airtight lids, these are ideal for storing liquids or semi-solid foods, such as casseroles and stewed fruit. They are also the best solution for freezing items that would get damaged easily in the freezer, such as a pavlova, cream cake or delicate pastry (paste) dish.

Note that when storing liquids or semi-solids, you can simply line the container with a polythene bag before adding the food, then remove the container when the food is frozen. You will need far fewer containers and will make the liquids into neat square or rectangular packs.

In the same way, when freezing a casserole or stew, you can simply line the casserole dish (Dutch oven) with foil, then pour in the cooked food and place the whole thing in the freezer. Remove the foil package from the container when it is frozen and wrap completely in a polythene bag. When ready to reheat it, remove the bag and foil and pop it back into the dish.

Interleaves

These special polythene sheets may be packed between layers of foods, such as chops, pancakes, etc., so they don't stick together. Foil or non-stick baking parchment can be used instead, or foods can be wrapped individually in clingfilm (plastic wrap).

Freezer tape

Tape is useful to seal bags or foil if the shape is awkward, making it difficult to wrap tightly enough, and to seal poorly fitting lids. Different colours are available, which you may use as part of your colour coding. Decorator's masking tape can be used instead of specialist freezer tape – and it's often cheaper!

Yoghurt pots and margarine tubs

Any tough plastic cartons with sealable lids can be used for short-term storage, providing the lids stay firm and they are scrupulously clean before use. If the lids don't fit well, overwrap in foil or a polythene bag or seal with freezer tape.

Toughened glass

Clean instant coffee jars and similar containers can be used to store loose, spoonable foods, such as breadcrumbs or grated cheese.

Twist ties or clips

Most freezer bags come complete with twist ties. You can buy a variety pack of different coloured ties if you are colour coding your food. Freezer clips may be bought separately and are good for sealing opened bags of free-flow foods, such as peas, but clothes pegs will do instead.

Labels

As we have already seen, it is vital that you mark what the food is, the quantity, the date and any special instructions for when thawed. Ordinary gummed labels won't do, as they won't stand the damp conditions; you must use self-adhesive ones with good sticking power. Freezer labels are widely available. Make sure you stick them on the bag or container when it is completely dry. If it's wet or greasy, they will come straight off!

Other equipment

Blanching baskets

Specialist freezing baskets are expensive and unnecessary. I use a chip basket for most vegetables (except small ones, like peas, for which I have a collapsible vegetable steaming basket). Alternatively, you can use a muslin bag – the sort you would use for straining jellies (clear conserves).

Freezer thermometer

You don't have to have a thermometer, but it is useful to check the temperature inside your freezer from time to time. It should stay at −18°C/0°F.

Serrated freezer knives

You don't have to buy special knives as long as your own are strong, good-quality ones. To saw through frozen food needs a rigid knife. A serrated knife will cut fish or baked goods such as whole loaves of bread. For large joints of meat or other tougher jobs, I use a sterilised hacksaw, suitable for cutting thick wood (pour boiling water over the blade before use – and clean thoroughly afterwards).

Removing the air from packages

This is vital to prevent oxidation. When you've put the food in the bag, gently squeeze the bag from the base up so that it fits closely over the food, then hold the bag and tie firmly. Alternatively, tie the bag loosely with a twist tie, insert a drinking straw and suck out the air, then quickly tie it securely without letting any air back in.

For rigid plastic containers, put on the lid, then lift it up at one corner. Press and squeeze out as much air as possible, then snap the lid shut so that it is sealed completely.

freezing principles

The purpose of freezing fresh food is to preserve it for later use. Freezing saves money because you can buy fresh produce such as fruit, vegetables or even meat in bulk (buying a quarter, half or whole animal is much cheaper than a single joint) when it is cheap and in season. It also enables you to enjoy specialities out of season and to make the most of foods on special offer or reduced for quick sale because they are nearing their sell-by date.

Tips for perfect frozen food

* Freeze only top-quality produce. Old, damaged or over-ripe foods will deteriorate quickly and won't improve with freezing.
* Food hygiene is vital. Prepare and freeze raw foods separately from cooked.
* Make sure you, your work surfaces and any containers and utensils used are scrupulously clean.
* Cool cooked and blanched foods for freezing as quickly as possible to room temperature before putting them in the freezer. Keep them covered while they cool.
* Fat deteriorates more quickly than lean meat, so remove all excess before freezing raw meat. Blot surfaces of casseroles or stews with kitchen paper (paper towels) to remove any excess fat or oil and drain fried (sautéed) foods on kitchen paper before cooling and freezing.
* Wrap foods properly and exclude as much air as possible from the packs – see pages 17–20 for more details.
* Don't be tempted to freeze foods that specifically say they are not suitable. There will be a good reason for this: either they will spoil – for example, single (light) cream will curdle on thawing – or they have already been frozen and thawed once (see below). This applies frequently to fish.
* In general, you should never thaw foods and then return them to the freezer without cooking first or you may get food poisoning. There are a few exceptions, however (see Re-freezing, page 197).

* Don't overload your freezer. Chest models have a clearly marked capacity line and food should not be stored above this. If you have an upright model, don't cram foods in until the drawers won't shut properly. If you do, the freezer won't be able to maintain the correct temperature and food will deteriorate. You'll also use far more electricity as the freezer struggles to work properly.
* Keep your freezer free from frost, which will naturally build up inside the cabinet. Use a plastic spatula to scrape off small amounts around the door or lid and when the frost is about 5 mm/¼ in thick inside, defrost the freezer. If you do not, it can't work properly.

What not to freeze

Most foods can be frozen, although, of course, there is little point in freezing some items – preserved foods, such as pickles, those with a long shelf life, such as dried beans and pasta and so on. But you should not assume that everything else will freeze successfully.

As I have already said, most previously frozen foods should not be frozen. There are exceptions (see Re-freezing, page 197) but as a rule, thawed raw foods need to be cooked before re-freezing. Thawed cooked dishes should not be refrozen – especially those containing meat, fish or poultry.

There are also a few foods that cannot be frozen, because the results are unpalatable.

Caviar: Becomes watery.

Cottage cheese: Becomes watery and chewy.

Cream with less than 40 per cent fat content: Curdles when thawed.

Cream cheese with less than 40 per cent fat content: Goes grainy and watery.

Custard: Only the canned variety will freeze successfully!

Egg-based sauces, such as Hollandaise, Béarnaise: Curdle when thawed.

Eggs, in their shells: Will expand and explode.

Eggs, hard-boiled (hard-cooked): Will go rubbery.

Garlic: Tastes musty when thawed on its own or used in large quantities for flavouring.

Jam (conserve): Tends to become runny – so in a jam sponge, for instance, it will soak into the cake.

Jelly (jello) and aspic: Will crack and go cloudy when thawed.

Mayonnaise and mayonnaise-based dressings: Will separate or curdle when thawed.

Pasta, plain, completely cooked: Becomes unpleasantly soft; may be frozen if undercooked, however.

Potatoes, old, boiled: Become watery. Some varieties will freeze, however – see individual entries.

Salad stuffs, such as cucumber, lettuce, radishes: Will go limp and mushy because of their high water content. Can be frozen if they are prepared for cooking – see individual entries.

Yoghurt: Plain varieties will separate when thawed. Fruit flavours can be frozen, as can yoghurt in a made-up dish.

Emergency freezing – fruit and vegetables

For good results when freezing foods for any length of time, it is vital you follow the preparation instructions in this book. But there will be times when you find that you have some fresh fruit or vegetables you just want to keep for a few days over their use-by date. These can be frozen just as they are, without any special preparation, such as blanching, but only for up to a week.

Ideally, chop or slice them before you freeze. For example, string and slice runner beans, separate cauliflower into florets, shred cabbage, hull strawberries and slice peaches. Place in a plastic bag, foil or a rigid container, seal, label and freeze. Pre-packed fruit and vegetables can be frozen just as they are. When you use them a few days later, they will be a little flabby when thawed, so stew fruits, adding sugar to taste, and cook vegetables from frozen. Don't leave them in the freezer for more than a week or the results will be very disappointing.

Fast freezing

The 'fast freeze' switch works by overriding the thermostat so the temperature drops well below the standard −18°C/0°F. Food that is fast frozen will have a better texture because the ice crystals formed in the food will be smaller, so less likely to damage the texture. This is particularly important with delicate foods, like fish. It should always be used if you are freezing a lot of food at once, perhaps if you have spent the day batch baking, or when you buy a quarter of an animal or have a glut of fruit or vegetables to freeze.

Some freezers have a special fast-freeze section. You should use this for freezing your foods initially, then transfer them to other parts of the freezer once hard.

To use the 'fast freeze' facility: If freezing a lot of food, switch it on up to 6 hours before you plan to freeze the food and leave it on for 12–24 hours. For smaller quantities, turn it on 2 hours before freezing and leave it on for 3–4 hours after freezing. DON'T FORGET to switch it off when the time is up. (I always put a note on the front of the freezer to remind me).

Thawing and cooking from frozen

For best results is to thaw food as slowly as possible. Thaw items in the fridge rather than at room temperature. If time doesn't allow this, see below for the different techniques.

Once the food has been defrosted, it should be cooked or eaten immediately. NEVER leave food lying around once defrosted.

When food is frozen, it inhibits any micro-organisms growing in the food but it doesn't destroy them. So when the food is getting nicely warm again, they come alive and multiply very rapidly. Consequently, to avoid problems, you should always keep food chilled, cook thoroughly as soon as possible, then eat immediately. When cooking and reheating, food must be piping hot throughout to kill the organisms. If you simply warm it, you are creating a nest of growing bugs!

Slow defrosting in the fridge

Remove foods from the freezer and place in the fridge still in their wrappers.

Make sure you allow plenty of time for thawing – up to 6 hours per 450 g/1 lb of food.

Meat, poultry, fish, juicy fruits and some vegetables may leak as they thaw, so put these items on a plate or in a shallow dish to catch any drips.

Defrosting at room temperature

It is sometimes necessary to thaw at room temperature but there is a danger of impairing the texture and flavour of the food, particularly meat, fish, poultry and game. Bread, cakes and other baked goods will defrost perfectly.

Compared to slow thawing in the fridge, thawing at room temperature cuts the time by about a half, which can be essential if time is short.

To speed the process of thawing meat or poultry up further, place the frozen food in its polythene bag or sealed plastic container in a bowl of cold water or under cold, running water. NEVER put in hot water. Although this method is not ideal, it's better than cooking from frozen.

Defrosting in the microwave

Thawing food in a microwave is quick, economical and hygienic and won't impair the texture or flavour as long as you follow the guidelines below.

Thawing is usually carried out at Medium–low (30 per cent power). Unlike when cooking on Full Power, the timing varies very little whatever the output of your model. You will find specific times for different foods in the second half of the book. The rules for arrangement, size and shape of food apply to thawing and cooking and are also listed under each separate food category.

* Remove any metal twist ties or lids before thawing in the microwave.
* If thawing meat or other foods where you don't want to use the liquid that drips out, place on a microwave rack with a container underneath so the liquid will drip away from the food.
* Thaw in short bursts only, with standing time in between. If you microwave for too long, you'll start to cook the outside.
* Check food before the end of thawing time and remember it will continue to defrost during standing.
* When thawing minced (ground) meat, scrape off the meat as it thaws and remove from the oven. Free-flow mince can be cooked from frozen.
* Break up casseroles, soups or other foods frozen in blocks as soon as possible and move the frozen pieces to the edge.
* Ease pieces of food apart as they thaw to allow more even distribution of the microwaves. This applies to chops, diced meat, sliced bread, bacon rashers (slices), etc.
* If thawing food in a bag, flex the bag occasionally to distribute the microwaves evenly.
* Don't try to defrost whole joints or poultry completely. Start the process in the microwave, then leave at room temperature, wrapped in foil, shiny side in, to finish thawing. Salmonella, a nasty form of food poisoning, can occur if the flesh starts to cook before it is completely thawed. Poultry portions, steaks and chops can be thawed completely by microwaving, however.
* Protect bone ends and thin ends of meat, poultry or fish with tiny strips of smooth foil as they thaw, to protect them from beginning to cook while the rest of the food completes thawing. Don't use large pieces or arcing will occur (sparks that could damage the microwave).
* Put cakes, bread and desserts on a piece of kitchen paper (paper towel) to absorb moisture as they thaw.

* Don't try to defrost cream desserts, such as cheesecakes, completely. Start the process in the microwave, and then let them completely thaw at room temperature.
* Vegetables can be cooked straight from frozen. Bags of frozen peas, for instance, can be cooked in their bag, flexing it now and then to distribute the heat.

Cooking from frozen

Throughout the book you will be told which foods can be cooked from frozen and which must be thawed first. Here's a quick reference guide.

May be cooked from frozen:

* Soups.
* Fish fillets, steaks and small whole fish.
* Shellfish, when added towards the end of cooking a hot dish.
* Chops, steaks, sausages and free-flow minced (ground) meat.
* Stews and casseroles (but they are still better thawed first for a better texture).
* Pasta and rice.
* Vegetables.
* Fruit for stewing, fruit pies and other cooked desserts.
* Bread and rolls (but they are best thawed first).

Do not cook from frozen:

* Any poultry or game birds.
* Joints of meat, especially pork.
* Offal.
* Soufflés.
* Uncooked bread dough or cakes.
* Fruit to be eaten plain in its juice.
* Cooked, made-up dishes (although they can be cooked from frozen if absolutely necessary).

a to z of freezing

This section tells you exactly how to freeze every type of food so that they remain in the best possible condition. You will also find lots of useful tips and information on equipment and freezer management.

a

Almond paste

Almond paste, or marzipan, does not need to be frozen. An unopened pack can be stored for months in the larder. If opened, put it in an airtight container and store it in the fridge.

Aluminium foil   *See* **Foil**

Apples

Any apples suitable for cooking can be frozen. Select fruit free from bruises or other damage. Avoid any with wrinkled or discoloured skin.

To prepare

Peel, core, slice and place in a bowl of water with 15 ml/1 tbsp lemon juice added to prevent browning.

To freeze

Dry-freezing, unsweetened: Drain and blanch in boiling water for 1 minute. Drain, plunge immediately in a bowl of iced water to cool, then drain again and pat dry on kitchen paper (paper towels). Pack into rigid containers or polythene bags. Remove the air. Seal, label and freeze.
STORAGE TIME: 9 months

Dry-freezing, sweetened: Drain and blanch in boiling water for 1 minute. Drain, plunge immediately in a bowl of iced water to cool, then drain again and pat dry on kitchen paper. Mix with caster (superfine) sugar, using 100 g/4 oz/½ cup to 450 g/1 lb fruit. Pack into rigid containers or polythene bags. Remove the air. Seal, label and freeze.
STORAGE TIME: 10 months

Purée-freezing: Stew the fruit in a pan with just enough water to cover the base, until pulpy. Sweeten to taste. Beat with a wooden spoon until smooth, purée in a blender or food processor or rub it through a sieve (strainer). Leave to cool. Place in polythene bags, remove the air, seal, label and freeze.
STORAGE TIME: 12 months

Syrup-freezing: Make a light syrup: for every 450 g/1 lb fruit, dissolve 100 g/4 oz/½ cup granulated sugar in 300 ml/½ pt/1¼ cups boiling water. Allow to cool. Prepare the apples, place in rigid containers and pour just enough syrup over to cover. Cover, seal, label and freeze. Alternatively, poach the apple slices in the syrup for 2–3 minutes until just tender but still holding their shape, then cool, pack and store as before.
STORAGE TIME: 12 months

To thaw and serve
Allow to defrost at room temperature for 2 hours before use. Apple purée can be reheated from frozen for apple sauce.

Apple pie *See* **Pies**

Apricots
Select ripe fruit with unblemished skins. They should give slightly when squeezed but should not be too soft.

To prepare
If you wish to peel the fruit, plunge in boiling water for 30 seconds, drain, then peel off the skins. Alternatively, halve and remove the stones (pits). Brush the flesh with lemon juice to prevent browning.

To freeze
Dry-freezing, sweetened: Mix with 100 g/4 oz/½ cup caster (superfine) sugar per 450 g/1 lb fruit. Pack into rigid containers or polythene bags, remove the air, seal, label and freeze.
STORAGE TIME: 12 months
Purée-freezing: Put the apricots in a bowl of boiling water for 30 seconds. Drain and peel off the skins. Halve, remove the stones, then stew with just enough water to cover the base of the pan until very soft. Purée in a blender or food processor or rub through a sieve (strainer). Sweeten to taste. Leave until cold, then pack in polythene bags, remove the air, seal, label and freeze.
STORAGE TIME: 12 months
Syrup-freezing: Make a light syrup: for every 450 g/1 lb fruit, dissolve 100 g/4 oz/½ cup granulated sugar in 300 ml/½ pt/1¼ cups boiling water. Allow to cool. Prepare the apricots, place in rigid containers and pour just enough syrup over to cover. Cover, remove the air, seal, label and freeze.

Alternatively, poach the fruit halves in the syrup for 2–3 minutes until just tender but still holding their shape, then leave to cool. Pack and store as before.
STORAGE TIME: 12 months

To thaw and serve
Thaw in the fridge overnight, then use as required. If serving apricot purée hot, it can be reheated from frozen.

Artichokes, globe
These are only worth freezing if you find some being sold cheaply (but still of good quality) or if you love them so much you want to eat them all year round. Select even-sized artichokes with rigid leaves, fairly tightly closed. Avoid any that are discoloured or damaged, look withered or have very open leaves.

To prepare
Twist off the stalks and trim the points of the leaves with scissors, if liked.

To freeze
Place in boiling water with 15 ml/1 tbsp lemon juice added and blanch for 6 minutes if quite small, 8 minutes if larger. Drain in a colander, plunge in a bowl of iced water to cool, then drain again and dry on kitchen paper (paper towels). Carefully open out the leaves at the top and remove the small inner, non-fleshy leaves and the hairy choke.

Wrap in foil, then place in polythene bags (this will prevent the leaves piercing the bags). Alternatively, pack in rigid containers. Remove the air, seal, label and freeze.
STORAGE TIME: 12 months

To thaw and serve
Cook from frozen in boiling, lightly salted water for about 5 minutes or until the centres are tender and a leaf will pull away easily. Drain and serve either hot with melted butter, pesto sauce or Hollandaise sauce, or cold with vinaigrette dressing or aioli (garlic mayonnaise).

Artichokes, Jerusalem
Select those free from excess dirt and with the fewest knobbles.

To prepare
Peel or scrub thoroughly. If very knobbly, I recommend peeling. Cut off any small knobbles – it may seem wasteful, but trying to peel round them takes

ages and they discolour quickly. Place immediately in a bowl of water with 15 ml/1 tbsp lemon juice added to prevent them discolouring. Thickly slice or dice and return to the acidulated water.

To freeze

Dry-freezing: Blanch the cubes or slices for 3 minutes in boiling water with a further 15 ml/1 tbsp lemon juice added. Drain, then plunge in a bowl of iced water to cool. Drain and dry on kitchen paper (paper towels). Pack in polythene bags or rigid containers. Remove any air, seal, label and freeze.
STORAGE TIME: 4 months

Purée-freezing: Cook the artichokes in boiling water for 15 minutes or until tender. Drain and mash with a potato masher or purée in a blender or food processor. Leave until cold. Pack in rigid containers or polythene bags. Remove the air, seal, label and freeze.
STORAGE TIME: 4 months

To thaw and serve

Cubes or slices: Boil from frozen in lightly salted water for about 5 minutes or until tender. Serve plain or mashed with a little butter and lots of pepper.
Purée: Reheat from frozen. Season to taste after heating and beat in a little double (heavy) cream or butter.

Asparagus

Select firm stems with a good, bright colour (green or purple and white). Avoid any that are flabby, wilted or slimy.

To prepare

Sort into thin and thick stalks. Trim the base of the stems if woody and scrape thick stalks.

To freeze

Blanch in boiling water for 1 minute (sprue or very thin stalks), 2 minutes (medium stalks), 3 minutes (thick stalks). Drain in a colander and plunge in a bowl of iced water to cool. Drain again and dry on kitchen paper (paper towels). Tie in small bundles and pack in polythene bags. Remove the air, seal, label and freeze.
STORAGE TIME: 12 months

To thaw and serve
Cook from frozen for 3–5 minutes in boiling, lightly salted water until the stems are tender but the heads are still intact. Serve hot with melted butter or Hollandaise sauce, or cold with vinaigrette dressing.

Aspic
Aspic, like any jelly (jello), does not freeze well; it will crack when thawed. If coating food in aspic, do so after thawing, before serving.

Aubergines (eggplants)
Select those with shiny unblemished skins and firm flesh. Avoid any that feel soft or have damaged skins.

To prepare
To peel the aubergines, blanch them whole for 5 minutes in boiling water. Plunge into cold water, then peel off the skin. Slice (peeled or unpeeled) more thickly than you would normally – about 1 cm/½ in – or cut into large dice.

To freeze
Blanch peeled slices for 1 minute, unpeeled pieces for 3 minutes, in fresh boiling water with 15 ml/1 tbsp lemon juice added. Drain, plunge in a bowl of iced water to cool, then drain and pat dry on kitchen paper (paper towels). Spread the pieces out in a single layer on a baking (cookie) sheet. Open-freeze on the sheet until firm, then pack into polythene bags or rigid containers. Remove the air, seal, label and freeze.
STORAGE TIME: 12 months

To thaw and serve
Cook from frozen in boiling, lightly salted water for about 5 minutes or until tender. Alternatively, thaw, then fry (sauté) in oil on each side until golden.

Avocados
Choose fruit that are just ripe – neither under- or over-ripe. If they are at all discoloured when you cut them open, don't freeze them. They can't be frozen whole, so are only suitable for made-up dishes once thawed.

The smooth variety should be shiny green and should give slightly when gently squeezed in the palm of your hand. The knobbly ones should be purplish-black all over but should not feel soft (the skin is much harder). Avoid any that are obviously bruised, have discoloured skins or feel very soft.

To prepare
Halve, remove the stones (pits) and scoop the flesh into a bowl. Add 15 ml/
1 tbsp lemon juice per avocado and mash well with a fork.

To freeze
Turn the mashed avocado into rigid containers, leaving 2.5 cm/1 in
headspace. Remove the air, seal, label and freeze.
STORAGE TIME: 2 months

To thaw and serve
Thaw at room temperature for about 2 hours, then use as soon as possible for
dips, soups, mousses or sandwich fillings.

b

Baby food, for infants

To prepare
Cook and purée different fruits and vegetables – see individual entries. Do not add any sugar or salt.

To freeze
Spoon into ice cube trays, wrap in a polythene bag, remove the air, seal, label and freeze.

STORAGE TIME: 6 months

To thaw and serve
You can offer the cubes individually at first, then 'mix and match' two or three different kinds to make mini meals. To serve cold, thaw in the fridge. To serve warm, reheat from frozen in a small cup in a saucepan of boiling water or in the microwave until piping hot, then cool to the required temperature.

Baby food, for older babies

To prepare
Cook and purée or mash foods, cover and leave to cool.

To freeze
Pack into small polythene containers or well-washed yoghurt cartons with lids, or seal with clingfilm (plastic wrap) if lids aren't available. Leave 2.5 cm/ 1 in headspace in the cartons.

STORAGE TIME: 6 months

To thaw and serve
Thaw in the fridge, then reheat in a saucepan, stirring until piping hot, then cool to the required temperature. Alternatively, heat from frozen in the microwave, breaking up the meal as soon as possible and stirring frequently until piping hot throughout. Cool to the required temperature before serving.

Bacon

Bacon rashers (slices) and joints are only worth freezing if on special offer and you eat them fairly often because cured meat with a high fat content goes rancid quite quickly. Select the leanest meat you can find.

To freeze
If bought loose, wrap firmly in clingfilm (plastic wrap), then foil. Label and freeze. If vacuum-packed, freeze as it is.
STORAGE TIME: 2 months

To thaw and serve
Thaw overnight, in the fridge if possible. Rashers can be defrosted in the microwave on Medium–low, peeling off the thawed ones as soon as they soften. Cook in your usual way.

If you think a bacon joint may be salty, thaw it in a pan of cold water overnight, then throw away the water. Boil in fresh water or roast in your usual way.

Bakewell tart

To prepare
Make in your usual way in a foil-lined dish or a foil container and cool.

To freeze
If made in a dish, open-freeze until firm, then remove the dish. Pack in a polythene bag, remove the air, seal, label and return to the freezer. If in a foil container, pack in a polythene bag, then remove the air, seal, label and freeze.
STORAGE TIME: 6 months

To thaw and serve
Thaw at room temperature for about 6 hours or overnight, then heat in a preheated oven at 180°C/350°F/gas mark 4 (fan oven 160°C) for 30 minutes. Cover loosely with foil if over-browning.

Baking parchment *See* **Non-stick baking parchment**

Bananas

These can be frozen only as purée to use in cakes, breads or desserts as the fruit will discolour. Use good-quality fruit that is just ripe – they should not be over-ripe.

To prepare
Peel and mash with 5 ml/1 tsp lemon juice per banana.

To freeze
Pack in rigid containers, leaving 2.5 cm/1 in headspace. Remove the air, seal, label and freeze.

STORAGE TIME: 6 months

To thaw and serve
Do not open. Thaw in the container in the fridge for about 6 hours, then use immediately to prevent further discolouration.

Banoffee pie

To prepare
Make in your usual way but mash the bananas with 10 ml/2 tsp lemon juice rather than slicing them.

To freeze
Open-freeze until firm, then pack in a polythene bag, remove the air, seal, label and freeze.

STORAGE TIME: 3 months

To thaw and serve
Unwrap and thaw in the fridge overnight, or at room temperature for about 4 hours, covered loosely so as not to damage the cream topping.

Baps *See* **Bread**

Barbecue sauce

To prepare
Make in your usual way and leave to cool.

To freeze
Pack in a rigid container, leaving 2.5 cm/1 in headspace. Remove the air, seal, label and freeze.

STORAGE TIME: 4 months

To thaw and serve
Reheat from frozen in a saucepan or in the microwave, breaking up the block as soon as possible and stirring frequently until piping hot.

Basic pie crust *See* **Shortcrust pastry**

Basil *See* **Herbs**

Bass

This is suitable for freezing only if the fish is very fresh. Check with your fishmonger that it has not been previously frozen. Select fish with bright eyes and gills, and a clean, fresh smell. Avoid any that look dull or have a strong smell.

To prepare

Clean and gut if necessary. Fillet the fish and cut into individual portions.

To freeze

Wrap portions individually in clingfilm (plastic wrap), then pack in a polythene bag. Remove the air, seal, label and freeze.

STORAGE TIME: 3 months

To thaw and serve

Cook from frozen in your usual way, allowing an extra 3–5 minutes' cooking time. Alternatively, thaw at room temperature for 2–3 hours and cook as soon as possible.

Batch baking

Large quantities of many favourite recipes may be frozen for use at a later date. Some items, such as shortcrust pastry (basic pie crust), bread dough and sponge cake mix, may be made up and frozen raw. Ideally, allow yourself a day – or at least the whole morning or afternoon – to have a freezer baking session. For best results, follow the guidelines:

* Always cool food thoroughly before freezing.
* Always label items correctly and include any special instructions for use when thawed, e.g. icing (frosting) a teabread or glazing a pie before baking.
* Always freeze in convenient quantities and put the quantity on the label.
* If you are freezing a quantity of whole dishes all at once, the freezer must be set to 'fast freeze' (see page 23) and, where possible, you should use the area of the freezer designated for fast freezing.
* Don't attempt to freeze more than 10 per cent of the total capacity of your freezer at any one time.

Sponge cake batch-bake mix

Makes enough for 1 gateau, 1 steamed sponge pudding, 1 baked sponge pudding and a tray of small cakes

  500 g/18 oz/2¼ cups softened butter or margarine
  500 g/18 oz/2¼ cups caster (superfine) sugar
  5 ml/1 tsp salt
  9 eggs, beaten
  700 g/1½ lb/6 cups self-raising (self-rising) flour, sifted

Put the fat, sugar and salt in a bowl and beat together until fluffy. Beat in the eggs, a little at a time, beating well after each addition. If the mixture begins to curdle, beat in a spoonful or two of the flour. Add a quarter of the flour at a time and fold in with a metal spoon, using a figure-of-eight movement. Use as required or divide into quarters, spoon into rigid containers, remove the air, seal, label and freeze.

STORAGE TIME: 3 months, raw or cooked

Basic shortcrust pastry batch-bake mix

Makes enough for 1 double-crust pie, 4 pasties plus a batch of tartlets or 2 large flan cases (pie shells)

  900 g/2 lb/8 cups plain (all-purpose) flour
  7.5 ml/1½ tsp salt
  225 g/8 oz/1 cup hard block margarine, cut into small pieces
  225 g/8 oz/1 cup white vegetable fat (shortening), cut into small pieces
  About 120 ml/8 tbsp cold water, to mix

Sift the flour and salt into a bowl. Add the fats and rub in with your fingertips until the mixture resembles fine breadcrumbs. Gradually mix in the cold water to form a firm dough. Knead gently on a lightly floured surface. Divide into quarters. If using immediately, wrap the remainder in clingfilm (plastic wrap) while you work with each portion. Otherwise, wrap the portions in polythene bags, remove the air, seal, label and freeze.

STORAGE TIME: 3 months, raw or cooked

Tip: When batch-baking pastry (paste), don't waste the trimmings. Roll them out and cut into attractive shapes. Place on a baking (cookie) sheet. Brush with beaten egg or milk and sprinkle with grated Parmesan or Cheddar cheese and a pinch of cayenne. Bake in the oven with your pies etc., for about 12 minutes until golden. Serve as nibbles with drinks or as an accompaniment to soups.

Basic bread dough batch-bake mix

Makes enough for 2 large or 4 small loaves, 6 rolls and 1 large pizza base

    1.5 kg/3 lb/12 cups strong plain (bread) flour
    15 ml/1 tbsp salt
    100 g/4 oz/½ cup butter or margarine, cut into small pieces
    2 sachets of easy-blend dried yeast
    900 ml/1½ pts/ 3¾ cups hand-hot water (or milk and water, mixed)

Sift the flour and salt into a large bowl. Add the fat and rub in with your fingertips. Stir in the yeast. Mix with enough of the water to form a soft but not sticky dough. Knead on a lightly floured surface for 5 minutes until smooth and elastic. Place in a large, oiled polythene bag, tie the end and leave in a warm place for about 1 hour until doubled in bulk. Knock back (punch down).

To freeze
Raw: Place convenient quantities in polythene bags. Remove the air, seal, label and freeze.

STORAGE TIME: Up to 1 month

Cooked: Shape, place in suitable oiled tins (pans) or baking (cookie) sheets. Leave to rise again for about 30 minutes, glaze and bake as required. Pack in polythene bags, remove the air, seal, label and freeze.

STORAGE TIME: 2 months

To thaw and serve
Raw: Thaw overnight in the fridge. Shape and allow to rise in a warm place before baking as usual.

Cooked: Thaw, still wrapped, at room temperature for 2–6 hours. If liked, crisp the crust in a hot oven at 200°C/400°F/gas mark 6 (fan oven 180°C) for about 5 minutes.

See also individual entries for cakes and pies

Beancurd   *See* **Tofu**

Beans, broad (fava)
Select fat pods with even-sized beans. Avoid any that look dull or are thin or discoloured.

To prepare
Shell the beans.

To freeze

Blanch in boiling water for 3 minutes. Drain in a colander, then plunge immediately into a bowl of iced water to cool. Drain well. Pack in polythene bags in convenient quantities. Remove the air, seal, label and freeze.
STORAGE TIME: 12 months

To thaw and serve

Cook from frozen in boiling, lightly salted water for 6–8 minutes until just tender.

Beans, butter   *See* **Beans, dried**

Beans, dried

All varieties of dried beans will keep for many months uncooked in a store cupboard so you don't need to freeze them. But it's worth cooking a larger quantity of dried beans than you need for one meal, then freezing the remainder for subsequent meals.

To prepare

Soak and boil in the usual way, but do not add any salt. Drain, rinse with cold water, drain again and dry on kitchen paper (paper towels).

To freeze

Pack in convenient quantities in polythene bags, remove the air, seal, label and freeze.
STORAGE TIME: 12 months

To thaw and serve

Thaw at room temperature for 3–4 hours, then use as required.

Beans, flat

Select beans that are firm and pale to bright green. Avoid any that are flabby or discoloured.

To prepare

Top and tail, then slice or cut into diagonal pieces, about 2.5 cm/1 in long.

To freeze

Blanch in boiling water for 2 minutes. Drain and plunge immediately in a bowl of iced water to cool. Drain again and dry on kitchen paper (paper

towels), then pack in convenient quantities in polythene bags. Remove the air, seal, label and freeze.
STORAGE TIME: 12 months

To thaw and serve
Boil from frozen in lightly salted water for 6–8 minutes until just tender.

Beans, French (green)
Select beans that have a bright green colour and will snap easily if bent. Avoid any that look wrinkly or discoloured.

To prepare
Top and tail, cut into short lengths or leave whole, as preferred.

To freeze
Blanch in boiling water for 2 minutes. Drain, plunge immediately into a bowl of iced water to cool. Drain thoroughly. Pack in convenient quantities in polythene bags, remove the air, seal, label and freeze.
STORAGE TIME: 12 months

To thaw and serve
Cook from frozen in boiling, lightly salted water for 6– 8 minutes or until just tender.

Beans, runner
Select bright green, unblemished beans that are firm and fresh. Avoid any that are wilted, discoloured or flabby.

To prepare
String and slice in your usual way.

To freeze
Blanch in boiling water for 2 minutes. Drain and plunge immediately into a bowl of iced water to cool. Drain well. Pack in usable quantities in polythene bags. Remove the air, seal, label and freeze.
STORAGE TIME: 12 months

To thaw and serve
Boil from frozen in boiling, lightly salted water for 6–8 minutes until just tender.

Beans, yellow

Select pods that will snap easily if bent. They should be waxy-looking with an even, creamy-yellow colour. Avoid any that are discoloured or flabby.

To prepare

Top and tail, leave whole or cut into short lengths, as preferred.

To freeze

Blanch in boiling water for 2 minutes. Drain and plunge immediately into a bowl of iced water to cool. Drain thoroughly. Pack in convenient quantities in polythene bags. Remove the air, seal, label and freeze.

STORAGE TIME: 12 months

To thaw and serve

Boil from frozen in lightly salted water for 6–8 minutes until just tender.

Beansprouts

These may be frozen for short periods only. They will not remain crisp on thawing so are only suitable for stir-fries. Choose very fresh, pre-packed varieties. Avoid any that are discolouring.

To prepare and freeze

As they are pre-packed, no preparation is necessary.

STORAGE TIME: 1 week

To thaw and serve

Cook from frozen, adding to stir-fries for the last 3 minutes' cooking time.

Beef

The colour is not a good indication of quality these days, since all animals for sale are young ones. But the meat should be very finely marbled with tiny grains of fat, and any fat on the outside should be creamy-coloured. Avoid any cuts that are very fatty or dry-looking with greyish fat.

If you have a large freezer, the cheapest way to buy beef is to buy a quarter of an animal. The hindquarter has the top quality meat – joints and steaks, mostly suitable for roasting and grilling (broiling) with a few for casseroling or pot-roasting. The forequarter, which is cheaper, is largely suitable for slower cooking – casseroles, stews and so on.

Whichever quarter you buy, tell your butcher how you want it prepared. For example, leg meat may be cut into dice ready for stewing or casseroling;

you could have the sirloin cut into some steaks, with the fillet separated and a piece left for roasting. If you aren't sure how you want it done, ask your butcher for advice. You can also get him to pack and label it for you in the quantities you require. For extra good value, take advantage of special offers.

To prepare and freeze

If you buy your meat pre-packed and labelled, there is no need for any preparation. Otherwise follow these guidelines.

Stewing or braising meat: Discard any excess fat and gristle and cut into dice or leave in portion-sized slices, if you prefer. Separate large quantities of unwrapped meat into convenient portions, if necessary. Pack into polythene bags, remove the air, then seal, label and freeze.

STORAGE TIME: 8 months

Steaks: Trim off any fat and gristle. Cover any bone ends with foil first for extra protection. Pack in convenient quantities into polythene bags, remove the air, then seal, label and freeze.

STORAGE TIME: 12 months

Minced (ground) meat: Shape into burgers or meatballs before freezing if liked or measure out useable portions for mince-based dishes. Pack burgers in rigid containers, interleaved with polythene interleave sheets, non-stick baking parchment or clingfilm (plastic wrap) to prevent them sticking together. Open-freeze meatballs on a baking (cookie) sheet, then pack in polythene bags. Pack loose mince into polythene bags. Remove the air, then seal, label and freeze.

STORAGE TIME: 3 months

Joints: Leave these as they are. Boned and rolled joints should not be stuffed until you thaw the meat before roasting. Pack into polythene bags, remove the air, then seal, label and freeze. Cover any bone ends with foil first for extra protection.

STORAGE TIME: 12 months

To thaw and serve

Ideally, thaw in the fridge for 5–6 hours per 450 g/1 lb, or overnight. You can leave the meat in its wrapper and there will be little or no blood loss. It is, of course quicker to thaw at room temperature for 2–4 hours per 450 g/1 lb.

Alternatively, defrost meat in your microwave on Auto-defrost or Medium–low, using the following guidelines.

Joints: Don't try to defrost completely in the microwave or they will start to cook before they thaw. Start them in the microwave, then finish at room temperature (see your manual for further details). Do not attempt to roast joints from frozen. Even if you like beef pink in the middle, you are unlikely to enjoy the result – the meat will have a well-cooked outer ring and a raw centre, rather than a gentle progression of colour.

Steaks: Separate as soon as possible during thawing in the microwave. These can be cooked from frozen, if you allow extra time, but the results may be disappointing.

Minced (ground) beef: Scrape mince from the block as soon as it begins to thaw and remove from the microwave so it doesn't begin to cook. Alternatively, cook from frozen: break up lumps of mince as soon as possible and keep stirring until no longer pink and all the grains are separate before adding other ingredients. Free-flow mince, meatballs and burgers can be cooked from frozen.

Diced or sliced meat: Separate the pieces of meat as soon as possible and spread out so they defrost evenly. Diced casserole or stewing beef may be cooked from frozen. Break up the pieces as soon as possible and keep stirring until browned and separate before adding other ingredients.

Pot roasts: Can be cooked from frozen, but make sure you seal the outside of the meat in hot oil before cooking to prevent all the juices running out.

See also **Casseroles, Curries** *and* **Meat, cooked**

Beefburgers *See* **Burgers**

Beetroot (red beets)
Select medium or small beets with little or no dirt attached. The leaves should be fresh-looking, not wilted.

To prepare
Cut off the leaves, leaving short stalks. Don't cut into the beets themselves or they will 'bleed' during cooking. Rinse thoroughly to remove any dirt, but do not peel or cut off the roots. Cook in boiling water for 10–25 minutes, depending on size, until tender. Drain, rinse with cold water and drain again and dry on kitchen paper (paper towels). Peel off the skins and cut off the roots. Leave small beets whole, slice or dice larger ones.

To freeze
Pack in convenient quantities in rigid containers or polythene bags. Remove the air, seal, label and freeze.

STORAGE TIME: 6 months

To thaw and serve

Thaw at room temperature for up to 4 hours, or in the microwave. Serve cold, plain or dressed with vinegar, vinaigrette, mayonnaise or soured (dairy sour) cream and chives, as a salad. To serve hot, reheat in the microwave in a covered dish or steam in a colander over a pan of boiling water for 4–5 minutes, then season to taste. Alternatively, add to a white, parsley or cheese sauce and reheat. Also use in soups.

Belgian endive *See* **Chicory**

Bell peppers *See* **Peppers**

Biscuits (cookies)

There is no reason to freeze packets of biscuits, as they will keep for months if stored unopened in an airtight tin. It is well worth freezing home-made biscuits uncooked, however; they can then baked from frozen as required.

To prepare

Make a biscuit dough according to your usual recipe. It may be rubbed in or creamed. Roll out and cut into biscuits and lay on non-stick baking parchment on baking (cookie) sheets. Alternatively, shape the dough into a sausage as fat as the diameter of the required finished biscuits. Creamed doughs – for Viennese biscuits, for example – can be piped into shapes on a lined baking sheet.

To freeze

Open-freeze sheets of uncooked biscuits until firm, then pack in rigid containers and remove the air. Wrap rolls of dough in clingfilm (plastic wrap), then overwrap in foil. Seal, label and freeze.
STORAGE TIME: 6 months

To thaw and serve

Thaw rolls of dough at room temperature, then cut into biscuit shapes. Place on a greased baking (cookie) sheet and bake at your usual temperature. Ready-cut biscuits may be cooked from frozen in the same way, allowing an extra 5 minutes' cooking time.

See also **Scones, Shortbread** *and* **Flapjacks**

Blackberries

Select ripe fruit with a shiny, bluish-black colouring. Avoid any that are over-ripe or greenish red.

To prepare

Pick over and discard any stalks. Wash and pat dry on kitchen paper (paper towels).

To freeze

Spread out on baking (cookie) sheets and open-freeze until firm. Tip into rigid containers or polythene bags in convenient quantities, remove the air, seal, label and store in the freezer.

STORAGE TIME: 12 months

To thaw and serve

Defrost at room temperature for 1–2 hours, then use as required. The fruit can be cooked from frozen for pies, fools, etc.

Blackcurrants

Select ripe fruit, still attached to their stalks. Avoid any that are under-ripe (reddish coloured) or mushy.

To prepare

Remove the fruit from their stalks by holding the stalk firmly and pulling it through the prongs of a fork. Wash and dry on kitchen paper (paper towels), if necessary.

To freeze

Dry-freezing: Spread out on baking (cookie) sheets and open-freeze until firm. Pack into rigid containers or polythene bags in convenient quantities. Remove the air, seal, label and store in the freezer.

STORAGE TIME: 12 months

Stew-freezing: Stew the fruit in a saucepan with 45–60 ml/3–4 tbsp water and 100–175 g/4–6 oz granulated sugar per 450 g/1 lb fruit until the fruit is tender but still holding its shape. Cool, then pack in rigid containers. Remove the air, seal, label and freeze.

STORAGE TIME: 12 months

To thaw and serve

Defrost at room temperature for 1–2 hours, then use as required. The fruit can be cooked from frozen for pies, fools, etc.

Black pudding

It's not worth freezing slices but a whole one can be frozen in its casing.

STORAGE TIME: 3 months

To thaw and serve

Thaw in the fridge overnight or at room temperature for 2–3 hours before slicing and frying (sautéing) or grilling (broiling) in your usual way.

Blanching

Blanching is essential when preparing vegetables for freezing. It destroys enzymes that would otherwise cause the vegetables to deteriorate quickly. Blanching helps to keep their colour, texture and flavour and to retain their vitamin C content.

Prepare the vegetables. Bring a large pan of water to the boil. Plunge up to 450 g/1 lb vegetables at a time into the water. A blanching basket (see page 20) is useful for this. Bring back to the boil quickly and boil for the exact recommended time. Drain immediately and plunge the vegetables into a bowl of iced water to cool them as quickly as possible. As soon as they are cool, drain and pat dry on kitchen paper (paper towels). Pack in polythene bags in convenient quantities. Remove the air, seal, label and freeze.

See entries for individual vegetables for details of preparation, and boiling and storage times.

Bloaters

Bloaters are herrings that have been lightly salted, then smoked without being cleaned first. They swell up slightly during this process – hence the name! Select firm fish with a good colour and smell.

To prepare

If you intend to cook the fish from frozen, gut before freezing. If not, they may be frozen as they are, then gutted before serving.

To freeze

Wrap individual fish tightly in clingfilm (plastic wrap), then place in polythene bags. Remove the air, seal, label and freeze.

STORAGE TIME: 2 months

To thaw and serve
Ideally, thaw in the fridge overnight, then gut. If they were gutted before freezing, they can be cooked from frozen. Brush with melted butter. Grill (broil) over a fairly low heat in your usual way, allowing an extra 5 minutes if frozen.

Blue cheese *See* **Cheese, blue**

Blueberries
Select just-ripe fruit with firm flesh. Avoid any whose juice is running.

To prepare
Pick over, wash and pat dry on kitchen paper (paper towels).

To freeze
Dry-freezing: Spread out on baking (cookie) sheets and open-freeze until firm. Pack into rigid containers or polythene bags in convenient quantities. Remove the air, seal, label and store in the freezer.
STORAGE TIME: 12 months

To thaw and serve
Thaw at room temperature for about 2 hours, then use as required. May be cooked from frozen if making a hot dish.

Bolognese sauce

To prepare
Prepare and cook in your usual way. Cool.

To freeze
Pack in suitable quantities in rigid containers, leaving 2.5 cm/1 in headspace. Remove the air, seal, label and freeze.
STORAGE TIME: 4 months

To thaw and serve
Defrost in the fridge or at room temperature for several hours or overnight. Reheat in a saucepan, stirring until piping hot. Alternatively, reheat from frozen in a saucepan or in the microwave, breaking up the block as soon as possible and stirring frequently until piping hot throughout.

Bread

Sliced loaves, pittas, naans, part-baked rolls and loaves, etc. all freeze perfectly. French sticks and other crusty loaves are only worth freezing to keep them fresh for a few days. If frozen for more than a week or two, the crust tends to flake off.

To freeze

All types of bread can be frozen, unopened, in their original wrapping. If already opened, place the bread in a polythene bag. Remove the air, seal, label and freeze.

STORAGE TIME: 6 months (see note above on crusty varieties)

To thaw and serve

Whole loaves and rolls: Thaw, still wrapped, at room temperature for 2–6 hours. If liked, crisp the crust in a hot oven at 200°C/400°F/gas mark 6 (fan oven 180°C) for about 5 minutes.

Sliced bread: Thaw, still wrapped, at room temperature for 3–4 hours. It may also be toasted from frozen.

Pittas and naans: Thaw individually at room temperature for about 1 hour. Alternatively, warm from frozen in a toaster, under the grill (broiler) or briefly in the microwave.

Part-baked rolls and loaves: May be cooked from frozen but add on extra time to allow for thawing, following the manufacturer's instructions.

Rolls and French bread: May be reheated from frozen. Wrap in foil and bake in a hot oven at 220°C/425°F/gas mark 7 (fan oven 200°C) for 10–15 minutes until hot through. You can also thaw bread and rolls, still in the polythene bag, in the microwave on Medium–low. Allow a few seconds per roll and up to 8 minutes for a whole loaf. To defrost and serve rolls hot after thawing, heat on Full Power for a few seconds per roll. Don't overheat or they will become leathery or hard when cooled.

See also **Batch baking**

Bread rolls, home-made

You can make rolls in your usual way and partially cook them, then freeze, to be cooked fresh when required.

To prepare

Make up the dough, prove, shape and prove again. Bake in a preheated oven at 230°C/450°F/gas mark 8 (fan oven 210°C) for 5 minutes, reduce the heat to 160°C/325°F/gas mark 3 (fan oven 145°C) for a further 5–7 minutes, until firm but still pale. Transfer to a wire rack to cool.

To freeze
Pack and freeze as before.
STORAGE TIME: 6 months

To thaw and serve
Cook from frozen in a preheated oven at 220°C/425°F/gas mark 7 (fan oven 200°C) for about 15 minutes or until crisp and golden on the outside and soft in the middle.

Breadcrumbs

To prepare
Use only stale bread – it should not be too moist. Drop a piece at a time into a blender or food processor until as fine as required. Alternatively, grate on a coarse grater.

To freeze
Pack in a polythene bag, remove the air, seal, label and freeze.
STORAGE TIME: 3 months

To thaw and serve
It should be possible to spoon out the quantity you need without thawing the whole pack. Use from frozen for stuffings, sauces, etc. Thaw at room temperature for 30 minutes if using as a coating.

Bream
Select fish with bright eyes and gills, firm flesh and a pleasant, fresh smell. Check with your fishmonger that they have not been previously frozen.

To prepare
Clean the fish, if necessary, rinse with cold water and pat dry on kitchen paper (paper towels).

To freeze
Wrap whole individual fish tightly in clingfilm (plastic wrap), then place in polythene bags. Remove the air, seal, label and freeze. Larger fish can be filleted before packing in polythene bags.
STORAGE TIME: 3 months

To thaw and serve

If whole, thaw in the fridge overnight or at room temperature for 2–3 hours before cooking in your usual way. Fillets can be cooked from frozen, adding an extra 3–5 minutes' cooking time.

Brie *See* **Cheese, soft**

Brill

Choose firm fish with a clean smell. Avoid any that appear wet or slimy. Check with your fishmonger that they have not been previously frozen.

To prepare

Gut, if necessary. Trim the fins and tail and scrape off the scales. Cut the fish into halves, fillets or slices.

To freeze

Interleave with polythene interleave sheets or clingfilm (plastic wrap). Pack in polythene bags. Remove the air. Seal, label and freeze.
STORAGE TIME: 3 months

To thaw and serve

Thaw in the fridge overnight, then cook in your usual way. Alternatively, cook from frozen, allowing an extra 3–5 minutes' cooking time.

Brioches

Brioches freeze well.

To freeze

If packaged, simply place the packet in the freezer as it is. If bought loose or the packet is opened, place in a polythene bag. Remove the air, seal, label and freeze.
STORAGE TIME: 4 months

To thaw and serve

Reheat from frozen in a baking tin (pan), covered with foil, in a preheated oven at 220°C/425°F/gas mark 7 (fan oven 200°C) for about 10 minutes until thawed and hot through. Alternatively, heat in the microwave on Full Power for 20–30 seconds per frozen brioche, checking every 10 seconds so as not to overcook. Alternatively, thaw overnight, still wrapped, at room temperature, before reheating for a few minutes in the oven.

Broccoli

Select firm, fresh, bright green broccoli. Avoid any that feel flabby or have even the slightest hint of yellowing.

To prepare
Separate into even-sized florets.

To freeze
Blanch in boiling water for 2 minutes. Drain and plunge immediately in a bowl of iced water to cool. Drain. Pack in rigid containers to prevent damage. Remove the air, seal, label and freeze.
STORAGE TIME: 12 months

To thaw and serve
Cook from frozen in boiling, lightly salted water for 5–7 minutes until just tender.

Brown lentils *See* **Lentils**

Brown rice *See* **Rice**

Brussels sprouts

Select even-sized, tight sprouts. Avoid any that are discoloured or opening.

To prepare
Peel off any damaged outer leaves and trim the stalk end. Sort into large and small sizes.

To freeze
Blanch in boiling water for 1½ minutes if small, 3 minutes if larger. Drain and plunge into a bowl of iced water to cool. Drain and pack in convenient quantities in polythene bags. Remove the air, seal, label and freeze.
STORAGE TIME: 12 months

To thaw and serve
Cook from frozen in boiling, lightly salted water for 5–8 minutes, depending on size, until just tender.

Buckling

Buckling are herring that have been salted, then smoked, usually ungutted. Select firm fish with a pleasant smell. Avoid any that are wet or appear to be drying out.

To prepare
Gut before freezing, if liked.

To freeze
Wrap individual fish tightly in clingfilm (plastic wrap), then pack in a polythene bag. Remove the air, seal, label and freeze.
STORAGE TIME: 2 months

To thaw and serve
To serve cold: Thaw in the fridge overnight, then serve with lemon wedges and brown bread and butter.
To serve hot: Brush with melted butter and grill (broil) lightly on both sides until hot through or fry (sauté) gently in butter. Serve with scrambled eggs.
Tip: Buckling can also be boned and pounded with butter, nutmeg and lemon juice to make a pâté. If you intend to freeze the pâté for later use, you must use fresh buckling that has not already been frozen. Re-freezing fish may cause food poisoning.

Bulghar (cracked wheat)

Bulghar is very quick to cook, so it is only worth freezing if you have made too much. Make sure it is completely cold before freezing.

To prepare
Cook in your normal way.

To freeze
Spoon into a polythene bag. Remove the air, seal, label and freeze.
STORAGE TIME: 6 months

To thaw and serve
To serve cold: Thaw overnight in the fridge or for 2 hours at room temperature, then add desired flavourings.
To serve hot: Place in a colander or steamer over a pan of boiling water for 5 minutes, stirring occasionally until piping hot. Alternatively, place in a covered container in the microwave for 2 minutes, stirring once or twice, until hot through.

Buns *See individual flavours, e.g.* **Currant buns**

Burgers

There are many types of commercial burger available for freezing. Make sure that you only buy in bulk those you know your family enjoys. If making your own, choose a lightly seasoned recipe – strong seasonings alter after freezing and some may actually impair the keeping qualities.

To prepare

If commercially made, no further preparation is necessary. If making home-made, follow the recipe in your usual way, seasoning only lightly.

To freeze

If commercially packaged, simply place in the freezer. If loose or home-made, wrap individually in clingfilm (plastic wrap), then place in a polythene bag or stack in a rigid container, interleaved with polythene interleave sheets, clingfilm (plastic wrap) or non-stick baking parchment. Remove the air, seal, label and freeze.

STORAGE TIME: 3 months

To thaw and serve

Burgers may be cooked from frozen. Brush with oil and grill (broil) on both sides until browned and cooked through or heat a little oil in a frying pan (skillet) and fry (sauté) until browned and cooked through on both sides.

Butter

Butter is worth freezing if it is on special offer or you are treating yourself to some farm-made.

To freeze

Leave commercially packed butter in its wrapper, then wrap in foil or a polythene bag. Fresh farm butter should be wrapped in greaseproof (waxed) paper, then placed in a polythene bag. Remove the air, seal, label and freeze.

STORAGE TIME: Salted 3 months, unsalted 6 months

To thaw and serve

Defrost in the fridge for about 4 hours or at room temperature for about 2 hours.

Butter (lima) beans *See* **Beans, dried**

Butternut squash *See* **Marrow**

Butters, flavoured
Freeze immediately after making.

To prepare
Prepare according to your usual recipe and shape into a sausage. Place on a piece of greaseproof (waxed) paper and roll up.

To freeze
Overwrap the roll in foil or place in a polythene bag. Remove the air, seal, label and freeze.
STORAGE TIME: 3 months

To thaw and serve
Thaw at room temperature for 5 minutes, then cut into slices and use to garnish meat, fish, etc.

C

Cabbage

Cabbage is available all year round, so there is no point in freezing it unless you have a glut in your garden. However, it is useful to have some frozen in a made-up dish – such as a red cabbage and apple casserole – or shredded, ready to make such a dish. Select very fresh cabbage with crisp, firm leaves. Avoid any that are discoloured or wilting.

White cabbage that has been frozen, then thawed is not suitable for coleslaw as it goes soft.

To prepare

Trim and quarter all varieties. Wash under cold water and pat dry on kitchen paper (paper towels). Finely shred hard white and red varieties. Cut green varieties into shreds 1 cm/½ in thick. If making a cabbage dish – like braised red or white cabbage – cook it in your normal way and cool it quickly.

To freeze

Raw: Blanch the raw cabbage in boiling water for 1 minute for hard red or white, 1½ minutes for green. Plunge immediately into a bowl of iced water. Drain and pack in polythene bags. Remove the air, seal, label and freeze.
STORAGE TIME: Red and white 12 months, green 6 months
Cooked: Put braised cabbage in convenient quantities in rigid containers. Remove the air, seal, label and freeze.
STORAGE TIME: 12 months

To thaw and serve

Cook red or white cabbage from frozen in boiling, salted water until just tender, or cook in a casserole (Dutch oven) according to your usual recipe. Green varieties should be cooked from frozen in boiling, salted water for 3 minutes until just tender, or stir-fried from frozen. Braised cabbage can be reheated gently from frozen in a saucepan or in the microwave on Full Power, stirring frequently until hot through.

Calamari *See* **Squid**

Cake mixtures, uncooked

Uncooked mixture for Victoria sandwiches freezes well. Make sure you freeze it immediately or the baking powder will start working, and it will lose some of its lightness. Whisked sponge mixtures don't freeze well as they tend to become leathery when cooked after thawing. Fruit cake mixture can be frozen.

To prepare
Line the cake tin (pan) with foil that comes 5 cm/2 in above the rim all round. Grease the foil. Make the mixture in your usual way and spoon into the prepared tin.

To freeze
Open-freeze in the tin until firm. Remove the tin. Wrap the block of mixture in the foil, then in a polythene bag. Remove the air, seal, label and freeze.
STORAGE TIME: 2 months

To thaw and cook
Unwrap the block of mixture from the polythene bag and return to the original tin. Fold back the foil from the top. Thaw at room temperature for 2–3 hours, then cook in your usual way, allowing an extra 3–5 minutes' cooking time as the mixture may still be very cold.

See also **Batch baking**

Cakes, fruit

Light fruit cakes freeze well. There is little point in freezing rich ones, such as Christmas cake, as they keep well in an airtight container – in fact they need storage time to mature, which they won't do if frozen.

To prepare
Make up your usual light fruit cake recipe, bake and cool.

To freeze
Wrap in polythene bags or rigid containers. Remove the air, seal, label and freeze.
STORAGE TIME: 6 months

To thaw and serve
Leave wrapped. Defrost at room temperature for 2–3 hours and serve as usual.

Cakes, sponge

Sponge cakes can be frozen with a buttercream filling. If you are proposing to fill them with jam (conserve), do it after defrosting as the jam tends to soak into the sponge when frozen. Home-made Swiss (jelly) rolls should be rolled in cornflour (cornstarch) rather than sugar before freezing. Ideally, they should be frozen unfilled, then filled when defrosted. Sponge flan cases are good to freeze as they go stale quickly once made.

To prepare
Make the cakes in your usual way, bake and leave to cool.

To freeze
If you are freezing several layers of a cake, interleave with polythene interleave sheets, non-stick baking parchment or clingfilm (plastic wrap). Wrap the layers for each whole cake in a polythene bag or place in a rigid container. Remove the air. Seal, label and freeze.

STORAGE TIME: 6 months (plain), 3 months (filled with buttercream)

To thaw and serve
Leave wrapped unless decorated. Defrost at room temperature for about 1–1½ hours for single layers, 2–3 hours for a filled sponge, 3 hours for a Swiss roll. Little cakes will take about 1 hour.

See also **Batch baking**

Camembert See **Cheese, soft**

Canned foods

You may wish to freeze canned foods if you've opened a can and have used only some of the contents. Canned fruit, vegetables, pulses, meat, fish and even custard can all be frozen successfully in a suitable container.

To freeze
Tip the contents of the can into a rigid container. Remove the air, seal, label and freeze.

STORAGE TIME: 6 months

To thaw and serve
Foods to be served hot can, generally, be reheated from frozen but make sure they are piping hot before serving. Alternatively, thaw at room temperature for 2–4 hours first. Fruit etc. to serve cold should be thawed in the fridge overnight or at room temperature for 2–4 hours, depending on the quantity.

Cannellini beans   *See* **Beans, dried**

Cannelloni

Cannelloni, or filled pasta tubes, cooked and ready to serve, freeze well.

To prepare
Prepare and cook the cannelloni in your usual way, then put it in a foil-lined freezer-to-table dish. Cool quickly.

To freeze
Open-freeze until firm, then carefully remove the dish. Wrap the cannelloni completely in more foil or a polythene bag. Remove the air, seal, label and freeze.

STORAGE TIME: 3 months

To thaw and serve
Unwrap completely. Return to its original dish. Ideally, thaw at room temperature for 4–6 hours. Cook in a preheated oven at 190°C/375°F/gas mark 5 (fan oven 170°C) for 35 minutes until piping hot. Lay a piece of foil loosely over the surface if it is becoming too brown. Alternatively, reheat in the microwave on Full Power for 10–15 minutes until piping hot throughout.

Capons   *See* **Chicken**

Capsicums   *See* **Peppers**

Caramel (caramelised sugar)
Caramel can be frozen when hard (to be used, crushed, for praline or decoration) or as a caramel sauce, thinned with a little boiling water after the sugar has been caramelised.

To prepare
Caramelise the sugar in a saucepan in your usual way. If you want hard caramel, pour on to a sheet of non-stick baking parchment and leave to cool. If you want a sauce, add water and stir until dissolved. Cool the caramel sauce quickly by placing the base of the saucepan in cold water.

To freeze
Hard caramel: Leave in a slab or break into pieces first. Wrap in clingfilm (plastic wrap), then overwrap in a polythene bag.
STORAGE TIME: 12 months
Caramel sauce: Pour into a rigid container. Remove the air, seal, label and freeze.
STORAGE TIME: 12 months

To thaw and serve
Thaw at room temperature for 30 minutes (caramel), 2 hours (sauce). Use as required.

Carrots
Carrots are usually cheap, so it's worth freezing them only if you have a glut in your garden, or if you like to use young carrots all year round or because you prefer to have a supply prepared, ready to cook whenever you need them.

Select young carrots with smooth, clean skins. The tops, if they are still attached, should be bright green and fresh-looking. Old carrots should be dry (not cold and damp) with smooth, clean skins and a bright orange colour.

To prepare
Scrape or peel in your usual way. If large, slice into rounds or cut into matchsticks or dice. Leave baby ones whole.

To freeze
Blanch in boiling water for 3 minutes. Drain and plunge immediately in a bowl of iced water to cool. Drain and pack in convenient quantities in polythene bags. Remove the air, seal, label and freeze.
STORAGE TIME: 12 months

To thaw and serve
Cook from frozen in boiling, lightly salted water for about 5 minutes or until just tender. Alternatively, they may be used from frozen in soups, casseroles and stews.

Cassata

Cassatas, or ice-cream bombes, are great to have in the freezer for special occasions. If you buy them ready-made, they should be transferred from the shop to your freezer as quickly as possible (preferably in an insulated carrier). For home-made ones, follow the instructions below.

To prepare
Make in your usual way, putting the mixture in a freezer-proof bowl or bombe mould.

To freeze
Cover the mould with foil, clingfilm (plastic wrap) or a lid, and freeze until firm.

STORAGE TIME: About 3 months (or depending on your particular recipe)

To thaw and serve
Remove from the freezer, dip the base of the bombe briefly in hot water, loosen the edge with a round-bladed knife and invert over a serving dish. Hold firmly and give a good shake. Lift off the container and serve immediately.
Note: Some bombes benefit from being removed from the freezer up to 15 minutes before serving – see your individual recipe.

Casseroles

Casseroles made with meat, poultry, game and vegetables all freeze very well. I always make double the quantity, eating one half immediately and freezing the other for a future date. You can also freeze any leftovers in individual portions for quick meals-for-one (but not if they have already been frozen).

To prepare
Cook your casserole in your normal way. Cool as quickly as possible.

To freeze
Line a casserole dish (Dutch oven) with foil, then add the cold, cooked food. Open-freeze until firm. Remove the dish. Overwrap the block of casseroled food in more foil or place in a polythene bag. Remove the air, seal, label and freeze.

STORAGE TIME: 3 months

To thaw and serve

Remove all wrapping and put the frozen food back in the casserole dish. Thaw at room temperature for 4–5 hours or in the microwave on Medium–low for 15–20 minutes, stirring frequently.

Reheat in a preheated oven at 180°C/350°F/gas mark 4 (fan oven 160°C) for about 30–45 minutes until piping hot. Alternatively, heat in the microwave for about 15 minutes on Full Power, stirring occasionally, until piping hot throughout.

Tip: Make sure you use a straight-sided dish to freeze a casserole or other cooked dish, if lining with foil. If the base is wider than the top, you won't be able to get it out once it is frozen!

Cauliflower

Select firm, tight heads with white florets. Avoid any that are discoloured, have yellowing leaves or have been trimmed to remove damaged bits.

To prepare

Separate into even-sized florets.

To freeze

Blanch in boiling water for 3 minutes. Drain and plunge immediately in a bowl of iced water to cool. Drain again and dry on kitchen paper (paper towels) and pack in useable portions in polythene bags. Remove the air. Seal, label and freeze.

STORAGE TIME: 12 months

To thaw and serve

Cook from frozen in boiling, lightly salted water for 5–7 minutes, according to size, until tender.

Caviar

Do not try to freeze caviar: it goes watery when thawed.

Celeriac (celery root)

Select firm, round roots with as few knobbles as possible, for easy preparation.

To prepare

Peel, halve, then coarsely grate or cut into thick slices or large dice.

To freeze

Blanch in boiling water to which 15 ml/1 tbsp lemon juice has been added, for 3 minutes for slices or dice, 1 minute for grated. Drain, then plunge immediately in a bowl of iced water to cool. Drain again and dry on kitchen paper (paper towels). Pack in convenient quantities in polythene bags, remove the air, seal, label and freeze.

STORAGE TIME: 12 months

To thaw and serve

Cook slices or dice from frozen in boiling, lightly salted water for about 5 minutes until tender, grated for 2–3 minutes. Drain and serve with melted butter or mashed with a little milk or cream and butter. Alternatively, use from frozen in soups, casseroles and stews. Thawed grated celeriac can be served as a salad, dressed with vinaigrette or mayonnaise.

Celery

Select firm, clean heads with either pale, creamy-white or bright green leaves (this will depend on whether they have been forced in the dark or not). Avoid any that are dirty or wilting.

To prepare

Trim off the green leaves and the root. Cut stalks into even-sized pieces.

To freeze

Blanch in boiling water for 3 minutes. Drain. Plunge immediately into a bowl of iced water to cool. Drain again and dry on kitchen paper (paper towels). Pack in convenient quantities in polythene bags, remove the air, seal, label and freeze.

STORAGE TIME: 9 months

Tip: Don't put too much celery in cooked dishes such as casseroles that you intend to freeze – the flavour becomes very strong when thawed.

Chanterais melon   *See* **Melon**

Chapattis

To prepare
Make in your usual way and leave to cool.

To freeze
Wrap individually in clingfilm (plastic wrap) or foil, then overwrap in a polythene bag. Remove the air, seal, label and freeze.
STORAGE TIME: 6 months

To thaw and serve
Heat from frozen in a hot, heavy based frying pan (skillet) or place on a baking (cookie) sheet in a preheated oven at 200°C/400°F/gas mark 6 (fan oven 180°C) for a few minutes until hot through, turning once.

Cheddar cheese   See **Cheese, hard**

Cheesecakes
Commercial cheesecakes can be frozen in their packaging, following the instructions on the packet. Home-made cheesecakes also freeze well.

To prepare
Line your tin (pan) or dish with foil, or use a foil flan dish (pie pan). Make the cheesecake in your usual way. Cool, if baked.

To freeze
Open-freeze until firm. Carefully remove the container (unless you have used a foil one) and place in a rigid container, or overwrap in foil and place in a polythene bag. Remove the air, seal, label and freeze.
STORAGE TIME: 2 months

To thaw and serve
Defrost in the fridge overnight. Decorate and serve as usual.

Cheese
Most cheeses freeze well. Hard cheeses, such as Cheddar, are best grated first as they can go crumbly on thawing, but they can be frozen in blocks of no more than 225 g/8 oz. Soft cheeses, such as Brie, blue cheeses and fresh, soft cheeses, such as cream cheese, can all be frozen in cut pieces or in their cartons.

Do not freeze cottage cheese: it becomes watery and chewy on thawing. Fresh Italian Mozzarella can be frozen, then thawed and used for cooking, but should not be thawed and served cold as it goes soft. Danish Mozzarella, which is a dryer cheese, freezes well.

See also individual entries, e.g. **Cheese, hard**

Cheese, blue
Freezing stops the ripening process of blue cheese, but if it is already over-ripe, it will be just as smelly when thawed!

Select cheese at its peak of ripeness; it should smell appetising. Creamy blues should be pale-coloured; hard blues – such as Stilton – should be marbled with blue but the white part should be pale and slightly crumbly. Avoid any that are going brown.

To freeze
Cheese bought ready-packaged, may be frozen as it is; if open, wrap tightly in clingfilm (plastic wrap). Place wrapped cheese in a polythene bag and remove the air. Seal, label and freeze.
STORAGE TIME: 6 months (3 months if very ripe)

To thaw and serve
Thaw overnight in the fridge. Bring to room temperature before serving.

Cheese, cottage
Do not freeze.

Cheese, cream
Full-fat cream cheese freezes well. Do not try to freeze low-fat soft cheeses with less than 40 per cent fat content – they will become grainy on thawing.

To freeze
Freeze, unopened, in its sealed container. Label clearly.
STORAGE TIME: 3 months

To thaw and serve
Thaw overnight in the fridge before use.

Cheese, curd
Curd cheese does not freeze well; it becomes grainy on thawing.

Cheese, hard (e.g. Cheddar, Double Gloucester, Monterey Jack, Edam, Parmesan)

Choose cheese that is in perfect condition. Avoid any that is drying round the edges.

To freeze

If vacuum-packed, no more packaging is necessary. Wrap blocks (up to 225 g/8 oz maximum) in clingfilm (plastic wrap) or foil, then overwrap in a polythene bag. Pack grated cheese in rigid containers, polythene bags or toughened glass jars. If grated cheese is moist and likely to stick together, pack in convenient quantities, or for grated free-flow cheese, spread out on a baking (cookie) sheet and open-freeze until firm, then pack into suitable containers, remove the air, seal, label and return to the freezer.
STORAGE TIME: 6 months

To thaw and serve

Defrost blocks in the fridge overnight, then bring to room temperature before serving. Grated cheese can be used from frozen in cooked dishes.

Cheese, soft (e.g. Camembert, Brie, etc.)

Soft cheeses freeze well. They will not ripen further while frozen, but if over-ripe before freezing, they will be just the same after thawing.

Cheese to be frozen should be just ripe. It should give slightly when pressed, have a clean smell and a white, bloomed rind. Avoid any that feel too soft, are going brown or have a smell of ammonia.

To freeze

If bought ready-packaged, leave in its wrapping. If opened, wrap tightly in clingfilm (plastic wrap). Place the wrapped cheese in a polythene bag. Remove the air. Seal, label and freeze.
STORAGE TIME: 6 months (3 months if very ripe)

To thaw and serve

Thaw in the fridge overnight to prevent it from going too runny. Bring to room temperature just before serving.

Cherries

Select even-coloured, plump fruit. Avoid any that are shrivelled or damaged.

To prepare
Wash and dry the fruit. Remove the stalks, then stone (pit), if liked.

To freeze
Dry-freezing: Spread out on baking (cookie) sheets and open-freeze until firm. Pack in polythene bags or rigid containers. Remove the air, seal, label and return to the freezer.
STORAGE TIME: 12 months
Dry-freezing, sweetened: Add 100 g/4 oz/½ cup caster (superfine) sugar for each 450 g/1 lb fruit and mix. Spread out on baking sheets and open-freeze until firm. Pack in polythene bags or rigid containers. Remove the air, seal, label and return to the freezer.
STORAGE TIME: 12 months

To thaw and serve
Thaw at room temperature for 2–3 hours. Alternatively, heat gently in a saucepan from frozen until the juices run, then cook very gently for 2–5 minutes until just tender but still holding their shape. Sweeten and add lemon juice to taste. (They are especially good laced with brandy or kirsch!)

Chestnuts

Chestnuts can be frozen whole or as a purée. Leftover canned chestnuts may be packed and frozen as below (no preparation is necessary). Select shiny-skinned nuts that feel heavy for their size. Avoid any that are discoloured or smell musty.

To prepare
Make a small nick in the shell of each nut with a sharp pointed knife. Put the chestnuts in their shells in a saucepan of cold water. Bring to the boil, then remove the pan from the heat. Lift out the nuts, one at a time, with a draining spoon and quickly peel off the shell and brown inner skin. If the water cools, heat it again or the inner brown skins will be impossible to remove.

To freeze
Whole shelled: Pack in convenient quantities in polythene bags or in rigid containers. Remove the air, seal, label and freeze.
STORAGE TIME: 6 months

Purée-freezing, unsweetened: Purée the nuts in a blender or food processor. Put in convenient quantities into rigid containers, leaving 2.5 cm/ 1 in headspace. Remove the air. Seal, label and freeze.
STORAGE TIME: 6 months

Purée-freezing, sweetened: Weigh the shelled nuts. Purée them in a blender or food processor, adding 15–30 ml/1–2 tbsp caster (superfine) sugar per 100 g/4 oz/1 cup nuts. Spoon convenient quantities into rigid containers, leaving 2.5 cm/1 in headspace, remove the air, seal, label and freeze.
STORAGE TIME: 6 months

To thaw and serve

Thaw at room temperature for 2–3 hours. Toss whole chestnuts in melted butter and serve on their own or with Brussels sprouts. Alternatively, wrap each nut in half a rasher (slice) of streaky bacon and grill (broil) until golden. Use unsweetened purée for stuffings, sauces, dips and nut roasts. Use sweetened purée for desserts such as Mont Blanc.

Chicken, cooked

Whole cooked chickens, chicken portions and boned, cooked chicken meat can all be frozen, as can made-up cooked chicken dishes.

To prepare and freeze

Whole chickens: Wrap any bone ends in foil to prevent damage. Place in polythene bags, remove the air, seal, label and freeze.
STORAGE TIME: 2 months

Chicken portions and boneless meat: Wrap portions completely in foil, then place in polythene bags. Put cooked meat in a rigid container. Remove the air, seal, label and freeze.
STORAGE TIME: 2 months

Sliced cooked chicken breast: Cover in gravy, to keep it moist, and place in a rigid container. Remove the air, seal, label and freeze.
STORAGE TIME: 2 months

To thaw and serve

Whole birds, portions and meat: Thaw in the fridge overnight.
Chicken slices in gravy: Either heat from frozen or thaw first. Gently separate the slices as soon as possible and make sure they are piping hot throughout before serving.

Cooked chicken meat: If it is to be used for made-up dishes, you can use it from frozen but allow extra cooking time because it is vital it is piping hot through. I recommend you defrost it first to be absolutely sure.

See also individual entries for casseroles, curries and pies

Chicken, uncooked

Chickens vary in size from poussins (Cornish hens), weighing 450–900 g/ 1–2 lb, to capons, weighing up to about 2.75 kg/6 lb. Select firm birds with creamy-coloured skin. Avoid any that look very bloody, have areas of damaged skin or smell even slightly unpleasant. Any wrapping should be intact.

To prepare and freeze

Do not stuff a chicken before freezing. Simply truss, tucking the wing tips under and keeping the wings and legs tight to the sides of the bird. Wrap giblets separately as they will not keep as long as the chicken itself.

Ready-frozen chickens: Place directly in the freezer.

STORAGE TIME: 12 months

Fresh, ready-wrapped chickens: If you buy a bird like this from the supermarket, it may be placed direct in the freezer.

STORAGE TIME: 12 months

Fresh, unwrapped chickens: Remove the giblets and wrap them in a polythene bag. Undressed birds must be plucked and prepared: remove the head and feet, then draw it, discarding all the innards except the gizzard, heart and liver (the giblets). Cut off the neck and add to the giblets. Cover bone ends with foil. Wrap and freeze the giblets separately if storing long-term. Place in polythene bags, remove the air, seal, label and freeze.

STORAGE TIME: Birds 12 months, giblets 3 months

Fresh, portions and breasts: Wrap bony portions in foil before placing in a polythene bag, to prevent them from damaging the bag. Wrap breasts individually in clingfilm (plastic wrap) so they don't stick together, then place in a polythene bag. Remove the air, seal, label and freeze. Ready-frozen packs and fresh, sealed packs may be placed directly in the freezer.

STORAGE TIME: 12 months

To thaw and serve

Whole birds: Never cook from frozen. Ideally, defrost in the fridge for 24–60 hours, depending on the size of the bird, then cook in your usual way. If thawing at room temperature, allow up to 12 hours, depending on size, turning the bird over once or twice to aid the thawing process. Cook as soon as the bird has defrosted completely.

If you discover that the giblets were frozen inside the bird, remove them as soon as possible from the body cavity during thawing and place in the fridge until ready to cook.

Portions and breasts: Thaw portions in their wrapper at room temperature for 2–3 hours, then cook straight away. Alternatively, thaw overnight in the fridge before cooking. Never cook from frozen.

Chick peas (garbanzos)

Dried chick peas will keep for many months uncooked in a store cupboard so there is no need to freeze them. But when cooking a quantity for a recipe, it's worth cooking more than you need, and freezing the remainder for subsequent meals. Leftover canned chick peas can also be frozen as below.

To prepare
Soak and boil in your usual way. Drain, rinse with cold water and drain again and dry on kitchen paper (paper towels).

To freeze
Pack in convenient quantities in polythene bags, remove the air, seal, label and freeze.
STORAGE TIME: 12 months

To thaw and serve
Thaw at room temperature, then use as required.

Chicory (Belgian endive)

Chicory should be frozen only for use in cooked dishes as it goes limp when thawed. Select firm heads with white stalks and yellowish-green leafy edges. Avoid any that are browning or appear flabby.

To prepare
Cut a cone shape out of the base with a sharp knife, to remove any bitterness.

To freeze
Blanch in boiling water for 3 minutes. Drain, plunge into a bowl of iced water to cool completely. Drain again and dry on kitchen paper (paper towels). Pack in polythene bags in convenient quantities. Remove the air, seal, label and freeze.

STORAGE TIME: 6 months.

To thaw and serve
Cook from frozen in boiling, lightly salted water for 6–8 minutes until tender. Drain and serve with melted butter or Hollandaise or cheese sauce.

See also **Gratin dishes**

Chilli con carne

To prepare
Prepare and cook in your usual way, then cool quickly.

To freeze
Spoon into a rigid container, remove the air, seal, label and freeze.
STORAGE TIME: 3 months

To thaw and serve
Thaw either overnight in the fridge, or for 3–4 hours at room temperature. Chilli can be reheated from frozen either in a saucepan or in the microwave. Break the block up as soon as possible and make sure it is piping hot throughout before serving.

Chillies

Select chillies with firm, shiny flesh. Avoid any that are discoloured, damaged or shrivelling.

To prepare
Wash and pat dry on kitchen paper (paper towels). They may then be frozen whole to be prepared before adding to food. Alternatively, cut into halves

lengthways, remove the stalks, seeds and any membranes, then chop or slice.

To freeze
Pack whole chillies in polythene bags. Spread prepared chillies on a baking (cookie) sheet and open-freeze until firm, then pack into a polythene bag. Remove the air, seal, label and freeze.

STORAGE TIME: 12 months

To thaw and serve
Use from frozen. Prepare whole chillies as above while still frozen. When using ready-prepared, 2.5 ml/½ tsp is the equivalent of 1 medium chilli.

Chinese leaves (stem lettuce)
Freezing is only worth doing if the leaves are to be served as a vegetable, as they go limp when defrosted. Select crisp, firm heads with white stalks and greenish-yellow leaves. Avoid any that appear flabby.

To prepare
Wash, dry on kitchen paper (paper towels) and finely shred.

To freeze
Blanch in boiling water for 3 minutes. Drain and plunge immediately in a bowl of iced water to cool. Drain and dry again. Pack in convenient quantities in polythene bags. Remove the air, seal, label and freeze.

STORAGE TIME: 4 months

To thaw and serve
Cook from frozen. Boil in lightly salted water for 2 minutes until just tender but still with some bite, then toss in olive oil or butter and black pepper. Alternatively, use as part of a stir-fry, adding with the quickest-cooking vegetables, such as cucumber or beansprouts.

Chips (fries)
Ready-prepared frozen chips, for either deep-frying or oven-cooking, are an excellent freezer standby. You can also make your own.

To prepare
Cut up the potatoes in your usual way. Heat oil for deep-frying to 190°C/375°F or until a cube of day-old bread browns in 30 seconds. Cook the chips in large batches for 2 minutes until slightly softened but not browned. Drain well. Spread out on baking (cookie) sheets and leave to cool.

To freeze

Open-freeze until firm, then pack in polythene bags (they will be free-flow, so you can store a large quantity in one big bag if you prefer). Remove the air, seal, label and return to the freezer.

STORAGE TIME: 4 months

To thaw and serve

Cook from frozen. Deep-fry in your usual way until crisp and golden brown. Drain on kitchen paper (paper towels) before serving.

Chives *See* **Herbs**

Chocolate

Chocolate decorations can be frozen, ready to use at any time.

To prepare

Grate the chocolate or make curls or other decorations in your usual way.

To freeze

Place in a rigid container. Remove the air, seal, label and freeze.

STORAGE TIME: 2 months

To thaw and serve

Add the decorations to the cake or dessert while still frozen.

Chocolate cakes

Chocolate cakes can be frozen plain or iced (frosted). Home-made chocolate Swiss (jelly) rolls should be rolled in cornflour (cornstarch) rather than sugar before freezing.

To prepare

Make cakes in your usual way. Cool, cover or fill with buttercream or fudge icing (frosting), as required.

To freeze

Open-freeze iced cakes until firm, then pack in a rigid container. If you have several plain layers, interleave with polythene interleave sheets, non-stick baking parchment or clingfilm (plastic wrap), then wrap in polythene bags or place in rigid containers. Remove the air, seal, label and freeze.

STORAGE TIME: 6 months (plain), 3 months (iced)

To thaw and serve

Thaw at room temperature for 3–4 hours, then use as required.

Tip: When thawing ready-iced cakes, remove any wrapping while still frozen so the icing doesn't stick to the packaging as it softens and become damaged.

Chocolate mousse

To prepare

Make in your usual way in a freezer-proof serving dish. Do not decorate.

To freeze

Wrap the dish in clingfilm (plastic wrap), then foil. Label and freeze.

STORAGE TIME: 2 months

To thaw and serve

Thaw in the fridge overnight before decorating and serving.

Chocolates, assorted

Chocolates, particularly fresh cream truffles, can be frozen for use at a later date – a good idea if you don't want to pig out in one go!

To freeze

Place in a rigid container, remove the air, seal, label and freeze.

STORAGE TIME: 2 months

To thaw and serve

Arrange on a serving dish and thaw in the fridge for several hours or overnight, or at room temperature for 2 hours.

Choux pastry (paste)

Choux pastry can be frozen either raw or cooked.

To prepare

Make in your usual way, then bake, if liked.

To freeze

Raw: Pipe into balls, éclair shapes or a large ring on non-stick baking parchment on a baking (cookie) sheet. Open-freeze until firm. Pack in polythene bags or wrap securely in foil. Remove the air, seal, label and return to the freezer.

STORAGE TIME: 3 months

Cooked: Cool on a wire rack. Pack in polythene bags or rigid containers. Remove the air, seal, label and freeze.

STORAGE TIME: 6 months

To thaw and serve

Raw: Place on a baking (cookie) sheet) that has been well greased or lined with non-stick baking parchment. Bake from frozen, in your usual way, allowing an extra 5 minutes' cooking time. Cool and fill as required.

Cooked: Thaw at room temperature for about 1 hour, and cook in a moderate oven at 180°C/350°F/gas mark 4 (fan oven 160°C) for 5 minutes, or cook from frozen for 10 minutes. Cool on a wire rack, then fill as required.

See also **Eclairs and profiteroles** *and* **Quiches and gougères**

Christmas cake

There is little point in freezing Christmas cake, as it should be stored in a cool, dark place to mature before eating. Freezing will stop the maturing process. Even once cut, it will keep in an airtight container for a month or two.

Christmas puddings

Christmas puddings need to be kept for a month or two before serving to allow the flavours to mature and will keep in a cool dark place for a year. However, if you don't have these conditions, they can be frozen, after maturing, for use the following year.

To prepare

Make and steam in your usual way. Cover with clean greaseproof (waxed) paper, then wrap tightly in foil. Store in a cool, dark place for 1–2 months.

To freeze

Make sure the pudding is tightly wrapped in foil, then label and freeze.

STORAGE TIME: 10–12 months

To thaw and serve

Thaw in the fridge overnight or at room temperature for at least 4 hours. Steam for 3 hours. Turn out and serve.

Cilantro   *See* **Herbs**

Citrus fruits   *See* **Orange, Lemon, Lime, Grapefruit**

Clams

Canned clams can be frozen – useful if you have some left over. Fresh clams should be frozen only if very fresh and not previously frozen. Select fresh-smelling, closed shells. Avoid batches that have lots of broken or open shells.

To prepare
Canned leftovers: No preparation necessary. Tip with their liquid into a rigid container.
Fresh: Scrub the shells under cold, running water, discarding any that are open or damaged. Steam in a little boiling water in a covered pan until the shells open, shaking the pan occasionally. Discard any that remain closed. Strain the cooking liquid into a rigid container. Remove the fish from the shells and add to the liquid. Cover and leave to cool.

To freeze
Lay a sheet of greaseproof (waxed) paper over the liquid to protect the fish. Remove the air, seal, label and freeze.
STORAGE TIME: 1 month

To thaw and serve
Reheat from frozen in the cooking liquid, seasoning to taste. Strain and serve in a sauce or cooled and dressed with vinegar or French dressing.

Cleaning your freezer

Hygiene is very important so clean your freezer regularly. See page 12 for full details.

Clementines

Clementines are worth freezing ready for a quick fruit salad or when they are particularly cheap. Select sweet-smelling fruit that have firm skins and feel heavy for their size. Those that feel light or have loose skins may be dry.

To prepare
Peel, remove all the pith and separate into segments.

To freeze
Dry-freezing, sweetened: Pack in rigid containers in convenient quantities. Sprinkle each layer with 15–30 ml/1–2 tbsp granulated sugar. Remove the air, seal, label and freeze.
STORAGE TIME: 12 months

Syrup-freezing: Make a heavy sugar syrup using 350 g/12 oz/1½ cups granulated sugar to every 600 ml/1 pt/2½ cups water. Pack the segments in convenient quantities in rigid containers. Pour over the syrup to cover completely. Remove the air, seal, label and freeze.
STORAGE TIME: 12 months

To thaw and serve
Thaw at room temperature for 2–3 hours. Serve with breakfast cereals, as part of a fruit salad or in a trifle.

Cockles
Ready-cooked cockles can be frozen – useful if you have any leftovers. You are unlikely to find fresh cockles in their shells unless you collect them yourself. Loose, cooked cockles should be very fresh with little or no sand visible. (If the juices in the container they are being sold from appear to be sandy, the fish will be unbearably gritty.) Fresh cockles in their shells should be closed and undamaged. Avoid any with broken or open shells.

To prepare
Ready-cooked: Rinse well under cold, running water and pat dry on kitchen paper (paper towels).
Fresh: Scrub the shells under cold, running water, discarding any that are open or damaged. Steam in a little boiling water in a covered pan until the shells open, shaking the pan occasionally. Discard any that remain closed. Strain the cooking liquid into a rigid container. Remove the fish from the shells and add to the liquid. Cover and leave to cool.

To freeze
Ready-cooked: Place in convenient quantities in rigid containers. Remove the air, seal, label and freeze.
STORAGE TIME: 1 month
Fresh: Lay a sheet of greaseproof (waxed) paper over the liquid to protect the fish. Remove the air, seal, label and freeze.
STORAGE TIME: 1 month

To thaw and serve
Ready-cooked: Thaw at room temperature, then sprinkle with vinegar or French dressing and lots of black pepper.
Fresh: Reheat from frozen in the cooking liquid, seasoning to taste. Strain and serve in a sauce, or cool and dress with vinegar or French dressing.

Coconut

Coconut is best frozen grated or shredded. Choose coconuts that feel heavy and have a good quantity of liquid inside (give them a shake to hear how much there is).

To prepare
Bore two or three holes in the shell and drain off the milk. Split the nut into pieces. Remove the flesh from the shell and grate the white flesh or shred, using a food processor.

To freeze
Spread out on a baking (cookie) sheet and open-freeze until firm. Pack into polythene bags. Remove the air, seal, label and freeze.
STORAGE TIME: 6 months

To thaw and serve
Use from frozen in cakes and biscuits (cookies) or as a garnish or decoration. To make coconut milk, tip it into a bowl, cover with boiling water and leave to stand for 10 minutes. Strain through a clean disposable cloth or muslin (cheesecloth), lining a sieve (strainer), over a bowl. Squeeze the cloth well to get every last bit of the flavour out of the coconut.

Cod

Check with your fishmonger that the fish has not been previously frozen. The flesh should be firm and white with a clean smell. If whole, the eyes and gills should be bright.

To prepare
Clean whole fish, remove the head and tail and then fillet. Cut the fish into steaks or fillet portions, if necessary. Rinse with cold water and pat dry on kitchen paper (paper towels).

To freeze
Interleave with polythene interleave sheets or clingfilm (plastic wrap), then pack in polythene bags, remove the air, seal, label and freeze.
STORAGE TIME: 3 months

To thaw and serve
Thaw at room temperature for 2 hours first, separating the fillets or steaks as soon as possible, then cook according to your recipe. Alternatively, cook from frozen, allowing 3–5 minutes' extra cooking time.

Cod, smoked

Select bright-coloured fish with moist, but not wet, flesh. Avoid any that is drying at the thinner tail end.

To prepare

Cut the fish into portion sizes.

To freeze

Interleave with polythene interleave sheets or clingfilm (plastic wrap) and pack in polythene bags. Remove the air, seal, label and freeze.
STORAGE TIME: 3 months

To thaw and serve

Poach from frozen in milk or water according to your recipe, allowing 3–5 minutes' extra cooking time.

Coffee, fresh beans or ground

Vacuum packs are the best for freezing. You can also freeze loose fresh beans and ground coffee if they are very fresh. Freeze as soon as you get it home.

To freeze

If vacuum-packed, simply label with the date and freeze as it is. If in an unsealed pack, wrap tightly in foil, then place in a polythene bag, remove the air, seal, label and freeze.
STORAGE TIME: 12 months

To thaw and serve

For the best flavour, defrost for 2 hours at room temperature before use.

Coffee, infused

To prepare

Make strong coffee in your usual way and cool quickly.

To freeze

Pour into ice cube trays and freeze until firm. Tip into polythene bags. Remove the air, seal, label and freeze.
STORAGE TIME: 12 months

To thaw and serve

Melt in a saucepan or in the microwave. Use to drink or to flavour desserts and cakes.

Coley (saithe)

Select fish with firm flesh and a fresh smell. Make sure it has not been previously frozen.

To prepare
Ready-frozen packs may be placed straight in the freezer. Divide fresh fish into portion-sized fillets.

To freeze
Interleave fillets with polythene interleave sheets or clingfilm (plastic wrap), then pack in polythene bags, remove the air, seal, label and freeze.
STORAGE TIME: 3 months

To thaw and serve
Defrost at room temperature for 2 hours before cooking. Alternatively, cook from frozen, allowing 3–5 minutes' extra cooking time.

Collard greens *See* **Spring greens**

Confectioners' custard
Do not freeze. It tends to curdle or go grainy when thawed.

Conserve *See* **Jam**

Convenience foods
Convenience foods will always state on their packaging if they are suitable for freezing. Follow the manufacturer's instructions. If buying frozen, make sure you get them home and into your freezer as quickly as possible so they don't thaw out en route. Use an insulated freezer bag for transportation.

Cookies *See* **Biscuits**

Cooling
Cooked food should be frozen as soon as possible after cooking so needs to be cooled fast. Rinse cooked pasta or rice with cold water to speed up the cooling process. Stand pans of soup, casseroles, sauces, etc. in a bowl of cold water and stir frequently until cooled. Place cakes and other bakes on a wire rack in a cool place. Never put hot foods in the fridge to cool.

Coriander (cilantro) *See* **Herbs**

Corn *See* **Sweetcorn**

Cornmeal *See* **Polenta**

Corn kernels *See* **Sweetcorn**

Corn-on-the-cob

Young corn cobs freeze beautifully. Select cobs with an abundance of golden, swollen kernels. Avoid old cobs and those with withered ends or with any discoloured kernels.

To prepare
Trim the stalks and remove the husks and the silks.

To freeze
Blanch in boiling water for 5 minutes. Drain and plunge immediately in a bowl of iced water to cool. Drain and dry on kitchen paper (paper towels). Pack in polythene bags. Remove the air, seal, label and freeze.
STORAGE TIME: 12 months

To thaw and serve
Cook from frozen in boiling, lightly salted water for 10–15 minutes until the kernels will loosen easily. Drain and serve with melted butter. Alternatively, cook with a very little water in a covered dish in the microwave for about 3–4 minutes per cob.

Cottage cheese
Do not freeze.

Cottage pie *See* **Shepherd's pie**

Courgettes (zucchini)

Select small or medium-sized vegetables with brightly coloured, shiny skins. Avoid any that are discoloured or bruised.

To prepare
Trim the ends and cut into thick slices or sticks.

To freeze
Blanch in boiling water for 1 minute. Drain and plunge immediately in a bowl of iced water to cool. Drain, then dry on kitchen paper (paper towels). Pack in convenient quantities in polythene bags, then remove the air, seal, label and freeze.

STORAGE TIME: 12 months

To thaw and serve
Cook from frozen in boiling, lightly salted water for about 3–4 minutes or in the microwave with a very little water for 4–5 minutes, stirring occasionally. Alternatively, thaw at room temperature and fry (sauté) in olive oil or butter.

Couscous

Couscous cooks very quickly so there is little point in freezing it unless you want some ready-made for a party or have a quantity left over.

To prepare
Cook in your usual way and cool. Pack in convenient quantities in rigid containers or polythene bags. Remove the air, seal, label and freeze.

STORAGE TIME: 6 months

To thaw and serve
To serve cold: Thaw overnight in the fridge, or for 2 hours at room temperature, then add desired flavourings.

To serve hot: Place in a colander or steamer over a pan of boiling water for 5 minutes, stirring occasionally, until piping hot. Alternatively, place in a covered container in the microwave for 2 minutes, stirring once or twice, until hot through.

Crab

Only the freshest crabs that have just been boiled are suitable for freezing. Select a good-sized crab that feel heavy. Shake it gently: there should be no sound of water.

To prepare

Crabs may be frozen whole. Alternatively, pick out all the meat and keep the dark and light meat separate or dress according to your usual recipe.

To freeze

Whole crab: Wrap foil round the pincer ends, then wrap in foil and place in a polythene bag. Remove the air, seal, label and freeze.

STORAGE TIME: 1 month

Crab meat: Put the light and dark meat in separate rigid containers. Remove the air, seal. Place together in a polythene bag (for easier retrieval later). Seal, label and freeze.

STORAGE TIME: 1 month

Dressed crab: Cover with clingfilm (plastic wrap) and freeze until firm. Place in a polythene bag. Seal, label and return to the freezer.

STORAGE TIME: 1 month

To thaw and serve

Thaw in the fridge for several hours or overnight, then serve in your usual way.

Crabsticks

Fresh crabsticks sold loose have probably been already frozen and then thawed, so should not be frozen. Commercially frozen ones can usually be stored for up to 3 months – check the manufacturer's instructions.

Cracked wheat *See* **Bulghar**

Cranberries

Loose cranberries are good for freezing as the season is short. Select plump, shiny fruit. Avoid any fruit where the juices are running.

To prepare

Pick over, rinse with cold water and pat dry on kitchen paper (paper towels).

To freeze
Spread out on baking (cookie) sheets. Open-freeze until firm, then pack in polythene bags. Remove the air, seal, label and return to the freezer.
STORAGE TIME: 12 months

To thaw and serve
Thaw at room temperature for 2 hours or cook from frozen.

Cranberry sauce
Home-made cranberry sauce is delicious and can be made with frozen cranberries or from fresh ones when in season.

To prepare
Use 225 g/8 oz/1 cup granulated sugar and 250 ml/8 fl oz/1 cup water to 225 g/8 oz cranberries. Place altogether in a saucepan and cook until the fruit 'pops'. Turn down the heat and simmer for 3 minutes. Cool quickly, then pack in a rigid container. Remove the air, seal, label and freeze.
STORAGE TIME: 12 months

To thaw and serve
Either defrost at room temperature for 2–3 hours or heat from frozen in a saucepan or microwave, stirring frequently until thawed.

Cream
Cream with a fat content over 40 per cent freezes well. Do not try to freeze single (light) cream or reduced-fat varieties.

To prepare
Whip partially or fully before freezing. Sweeten, if liked.

To freeze
Partially whipped: Pack in convenient quantities in rigid containers, leaving 2.5 cm/1 in headspace. Remove the air, seal, label and freeze.
STORAGE TIME: 3 months
Fully whipped: Pipe as decorations on the inside of the lid of a rigid container. Open-freeze until firm, then press the base on to cover. Seal firmly, label very clearly and freeze, lid-side down.
STORAGE TIME: 3 months

Clotted cream, soured (dairy sour) cream and crème fraîche:
Freeze, unopened, in their sealed cartons.
STORAGE TIME: 3 months

To thaw and serve
Frozen cream decorations should be put in place while still frozen, then placed in the fridge to thaw. Defrost all other cream in the fridge overnight and use as usual.

Cream cheese *See* **Cheese, cream**

Cream soups *See* **Soups**

Crème caramel
Do not freeze; the custard will separate on thawing.

Crème fraîche *See* **Cream**

Croissants
Croissants freeze well.

To freeze
Because they get damaged easily, they are best packed in a single layer in a foil tray. Cover with the cardboard lid or foil, label, then freeze until firm. Alternatively, pack in a polythene bag, remove the air, seal, label and freeze.
STORAGE TIME: 3 MONTHS

To thaw and serve
Heat from frozen at 200°C/400°F/gas mark 6 (fan oven 180°C) for 15 minutes or in the microwave for about 30 seconds per croissant, turning once. Alternatively, thaw overnight in the fridge or at room temperature for 2 hours, then wrap in foil (unless you like your croissants crisp) and heat in the oven as above for about 5 minutes.

Croûtes and croûtons
Croûtes are slices of bread, often from a French stick or a loaf of ciabatta, fried (sautéed) or baked until crisp and golden for use as a garnish or as a base for canapés or starters. Croûtons, little cubes of fried bread, are ideal to keep in the freezer for use in soups and salads at a moment's notice.

To prepare
Cut bread into slices for croûtes, or small cubes for croûtons. Fry (sauté) in hot oil in a frying pan (skillet) or toss in oil and bake in the oven at 200°C/400°F/gas mark 6 (fan oven 180°C) until golden brown. Drain and cool on kitchen paper (paper towels).

To freeze
Tip croûtes into polythene bags and put croûtons in a screw-topped jar, then label and freeze.
STORAGE TIME: 2 months

To thaw and serve
Leave croûtes to thaw at room temperature for 2 hours before use or refresh in a hot oven as for preparation for 5 minutes, then use hot or cold. Croûtons can be used from frozen on hot soup or thawed at room temperature for 1 hour before adding to salads.

Crumbles, fruit

To prepare
Make the whole dish according to your usual recipe but place in a foil-lined dish. Bake, if liked, or freeze raw.

To freeze
Open-freeze. Wrap in clingfilm (plastic wrap), then foil. Label and freeze.
STORAGE TIME: 3 months

To thaw and serve
Thaw overnight in the fridge or at room temperature for 3–4 hours, then cook or reheat in a moderately hot oven at 190°C/375°F/gas mark 5 (fan oven 170°C) for 20–30 minutes or until piping hot throughout.

Cucumbers
Cucumbers can be frozen only for use in soups, sauces or cooked dishes because the high water content makes them very limp on thawing.

To prepare
Peel and finely dice or purée in a blender or food processor. Alternatively, stuff them or make a cucumber mornay (in cheese sauce) and place in a dish lined with foil, or make cucumber soup but don't add any cream.

To freeze

Dice and purée: Pack in convenient quantities in rigid containers, leaving 2.5 cm/1 in headspace. Remove the air, seal, label and freeze.

STORAGE TIME: 2 months

Cooked dishes: Open-freeze until firm. Overwrap in foil, then a polythene bag. Remove the air, seal, label and freeze.

STORAGE TIME: 2 months

Soup: Pour into a rigid container, leaving 2.5 cm/1 in headspace. Remove the air, seal, label and freeze.

STORAGE TIME: 2 months

To thaw and serve

Dice and purée: Thaw in the fridge overnight. Use purée to make soup. Drain dice thoroughly before adding to sauces.

Cooked dishes: Unwrap and return to the cooking dish if necessary. Thaw overnight in the fridge or at room temperature for 2–3 hours. Reheat in your usual way.

Soups: Heat from frozen in a saucepan or the microwave, breaking up the block as soon as possible, and stirring frequently, until piping hot. Add any cream before serving.

Curd cheese *See* **cheese, curd**

Curly kale

Select dark green leaves, avoiding any with yellowing edges.

To prepare

Separate leaves and remove thick stalks. Wash well in cold water and drain.

To freeze

Blanch the whole leaves in boiling water for 1 minute. Drain and plunge immediately in a bowl of iced water to cool. Drain again and dry on kitchen paper (paper towels) and shred. Pack in convenient quantities in polythene bags. Remove the air, seal, label and freeze.

STORAGE TIME: 6 months

To thaw and serve

Cook from frozen in boiling, lightly salted water for 6–8 minutes.

Currant buns

Currant buns – and all other types of bun – freeze well.

To freeze

Place in polythene bags, remove the air, seal, label and freeze.

STORAGE TIME: 4 months

To thaw and serve

Thaw at room temperature in their bags for 2 hours. Alternatively, thaw in the microwave on Medium–low for a few seconds per bun, then reheat for a few seconds per bun on Full Power. Alternatively, wrap in foil and bake in a hot oven at 200°C/400°F/gas mark 6 (fan oven 180°C) for 5–10 minutes until thawed and warm. If you have a serrated-edged knife, you can halve them while frozen and toast.

Curries

Curries freeze well, and the flavour can actually improve on thawing.

To prepare

Make the curry in your usual way. Cool quickly.

To freeze

Tip into a rigid container, leaving 2.5 cm/1 in headspace. Remove the air, seal, label and freeze.

STORAGE TIME: 3 months

To thaw and serve

Thaw overnight in the sealed container in the fridge, then tip into a saucepan and reheat until piping hot, stirring frequently. Alternatively, start thawing in the microwave in the container, on Medium–low, breaking up as soon as possible. Then tip into a microwave-safe dish, cover and heat on Full Power, stirring every few minutes, until piping hot throughout.

Custard

Don't freeze egg custards – they separate on thawing – or those based on cornflour (cornstarch) – they go lumpy. If you have leftover canned custard, however, this freezes well.

To freeze

Tip into a rigid container, leaving 2.5 cm/1 in headspace. Remove the air, seal, label and freeze.

STORAGE TIME: 2 months

To thaw and serve

Preferably thaw overnight in the fridge, then reheat in a saucepan or in the microwave, if liked.

d

Dabs

To choose
Check with your fishmonger that the fish has not been previously frozen. The flesh should be firm with a fresh smell. The eyes should be bright.

To prepare
Rinse with cold water and pat dry on kitchen paper (paper towels).

To freeze
Interleave with polythene interleave sheets or clingfilm (plastic wrap), then pack in polythene bags, remove the air, seal, label and freeze.
STORAGE TIME: 3 months

To thaw and serve
Trim the fins and tails. Thaw at room temperature for 2 hours, then cook in your usual way. Alternatively, cook from frozen, using your usual method and adding 5 minutes' extra cooking time.

Dace
Check with your fishmonger that the fish has not been previously frozen. The flesh should be firm with a fresh smell and the eyes should be bright.

To prepare
Rinse with cold water and pat dry on kitchen paper (paper towels).

To freeze
Interleave with polythene interleave sheets or clingfilm (plastic wrap), then pack in polythene bags, remove the air, seal, label and freeze.
STORAGE TIME: 3 months

To thaw and serve
Trim the fins and tails. Thaw at room temperature for 2 hours, then cook in your usual way. Alternatively, cook from frozen in your usual way, adding 5 minutes' extra cooking time.

Damsons

The skins of damsons tend to toughen after freezing, as they do when cooked. If this is unpalatable, purée the fruit (see below). Select ripe, unblemished fruit.

To prepare
Wash, halve and remove the stones (pits) or leave whole, if preferred.

To freeze
Dry-freezing, sweetened: Pack in layers in convenient quantities, sprinkling caster (superfine) sugar between each layer, using about 225 g/ 8 oz/1 cup sugar per 450 g/1b fruit. Remove the air, seal, label and freeze.
STORAGE TIME: 12 months

Syrup-freezing: Make a heavy syrup using 350 g/12 oz/1½ cups granulated sugar to every 600 ml/1 pt/2½ cups water. Pack the damsons in convenient quantities in rigid containers, leaving 2.5 cm/1 in headspace. Pour just enough syrup over to cover the fruit. Remove the air, seal, label and freeze.
STORAGE TIME: 12 months

Purée-freezing: Put just enough water in a saucepan to cover the base. Add the stoned (pitted) fruit, cover and cook gently until the fruit is tender, stirring occasionally. Purée in a blender or food processor or pass through a fine sieve (strainer) and sweeten to taste. Pour in convenient quantities into rigid containers, leaving 2.5 cm/1 in headspace. Remove the air, seal, label and freeze.
STORAGE TIME: 12 months

To thaw and serve
Thaw at room temperature for about 3 hours, then use as required.

Danish pastries
Because pastries can get damaged easily, it's worth taking the trouble to pack them properly. If iced (frosted), make sure the covering of the container does not touch the top of the pastry.

To freeze
Place in a single layer in a foil tray. Add the cardboard lid, if available, and seal. Alternatively, wrap in foil, then place in a polythene bag, remove the air and seal. Label and freeze.
STORAGE TIME: 3 months

Dates

Dried dates keep well in a cool dark place, so there is little point in freezing them. Fresh dates freeze well. Select plump, shiny dates and avoid any that are damaged or drying out.

To prepare
Halve and remove the stones (pits).

To freeze
Pack in convenient quantities in rigid containers or polythene bags. Remove the air, seal, label and freeze.

STORAGE TIME: 12 months

To thaw and serve
Thaw at room temperature for 2–3 hours, then use as you would if fresh.

Deep-freezing

Deep-freezing preserves food by reducing the temperature so that bacteria cannot grow and chemical changes are halted. However, freezing does not kill micro-organisms, it simply keeps them in suspended animation, so that as soon as the food is thawed, these processes start up again, and the food will deteriorate as quickly as before it was frozen. For this reason, food should be cooked and eaten as soon as possible after defrosting.

Your freezer should be kept at −18°C/0°F and food is fast-frozen at −25 to −30°C/−13 to −22°F. Commercially deep-frozen foods are blast-frozen at temperatures as low as −73°C/−100°F.

Defrosting your freezer

For optimum performance, it is vital you defrost your freezer once or twice a year. For full details, see page 13.

Delicatessen meats

Salamis and other slicing sausages don't freeze well because of their high fat and salt content but they can be stored briefly if absolutely necessary. They are best used in cooked dishes once thawed. Whole, dry salamis will keep well in the fridge.

To freeze
If vacuum-packed, freeze as it is. If sliced to order, interleave each slice with polythene interleave sheets, clingfilm (plastic wrap) or non-stick baking

parchment, then pack flat in a polythene bag. Remove the air, seal, label and freeze. Whole, dry salamis can be wrapped in clingfilm (plastic wrap), then foil or a polythene bag. Seal, label and freeze.

STORAGE TIME: 1 month

To thaw and serve
Thaw in the fridge overnight and use as required.

Dill (dill weed) *See* **Herbs**

Dog food *See* **Pet food**

Dolmas
Stuffed vine leaves and cabbage leaves freeze well.

To prepare
Make in your usual way. Cool quickly.

To freeze
Plain dolmas: Simply pack the rolls in foil, then place in a rigid container. Remove the air, seal, label and freeze.

STORAGE TIME: 3 months

Dolmas in a sauce: Place in a single layer in a foil-lined casserole dish (Dutch oven), then cover with foil and freeze. Remove from the dish and place in a polythene bag, remove the air, seal, label and freeze.

STORAGE TIME: 3 months

To thaw and serve
Plain dolmas: Leave in the container. Thaw in the fridge overnight and serve cold.

Dolmas in a sauce: Remove the foil and return the contents to the dish while still frozen. Thaw in the fridge overnight. Reheat in a hot oven at 200°C/400°F/gas mark 6 (fan oven 180°C) for about 20 minutes until piping hot. Alternatively, reheat in the microwave on Full Power, rearranging the rolls once or twice, until piping hot.

Dough *See* **Bread, Biscuits** *and* **Pastry**

Doughnuts

It is only worth freezing doughnuts if they are absolutely fresh (and remember, they go stale within a day!)

To freeze

Place in rigid containers or in polythene bags. Remove the air, seal, label and freeze.

STORAGE TIME: 3 months

To thaw and serve

Thaw at room temperature for 2 hours or in the microwave on Medium–low for about 45 seconds to 1 minute each, turning once halfway through defrosting. Be careful when serving doughnuts with jam (conserve), as it may get very hot when microwaved.

Dover sole *See* **Sole**

Dry-freezing

This is a very quick way of preserving fruit or vegetables without adding liquid.

Prepare the fruit or vegetables, then pack in rigid containers. Fruits can be layered with sugar, if appropriate. Remove the air, seal the containers, label and freeze.

See also **Open-freezing**

Duck/duckling

Duckling are birds under 3 months old, weighing up to 1.5 kg/3 lb. Ducks are up to a year old and weigh up to twice as much.

To prepare and freeze

Do not stuff ducks before freezing.

Ready-prepared, frozen ducks: Birds like this, bought from the supermarket, may be placed directly in the freezer.

STORAGE TIME: 6 months

Fresh, farmed ducks: These may be bought ready-prepared from the supermarket. Simply overwrap in foil or a stronger polythene bag. Remove the air, seal, label and freeze.

STORAGE TIME: 6 months

Undressed farmed or wild duck: If necessary, pluck and draw the bird, removing its head and feet. Reserve the heart, gizzard, liver and neck for stock. Discard the remainder. Wrap the giblets separately as they don't keep as well as the duck. Rinse the bird under cold, running water and dry inside and out with kitchen paper (paper towels). Truss the bird. Wrap bone ends in foil to protect them, then wrap the bird in a polythene bag. Put the bag of giblets in as well. Remove the air, seal, label and freeze.

STORAGE TIME: Birds 6 months, giblets 3 months

To thaw and serve

Thaw at room temperature for up to 12 hours, depending on the size or in the fridge for 24 hours. Prepare and cook in your usual way.

Dumplings

Dumplings cooked in a stew can be frozen.

To prepare and freeze

To prevent damaging dumplings when thawing and reheating the stew, remove them and freeze them in a separate rigid container.

To thaw and serve

Thaw separately at room temperature for about 2 hours, then return to the top of the stew when reheating.

e

Eclairs and profiteroles

These freeze well, with or without icing (frosting) or chocolate sauce.

To prepare
Make, fill and ice (frost), if liked, in your usual way.

To freeze
Iced: Pack in a single layer in a foil tray with a lid. Open-freeze until firm, then cover with the lid, seal, label and return to the freezer.
Plain: Pack in rigid containers, seal, label and freeze.
STORAGE TIME: 3 months

To thaw and serve
Thaw overnight in the fridge or for 2–3 hours at room temperature. Ice or add sauce after defrosting, if necessary.

Eels

Freshly caught eels freeze well, both freshwater and seawater varieties.

To prepare and freeze
Large freshwater and conger eels: Cut off the heads and gut the eels, then rinse thoroughly under cold, running water. Pull off the skin. Cut into short lengths. Pack in convenient quantities in polythene bags, remove the air, seal, label and freeze.
STORAGE TIME: 3 months
Elvers: Wash and freeze whole. Pack in convenient quantities in polythene bags, remove the air, seal, label and freeze.
STORAGE TIME: 3 months

To thaw and serve
Thaw at room temperature for 2–3 hours. Poach, or toss in seasoned flour and fry (sauté), or brush with oil and grill (broil) or barbecue.

Egg custard
Do not freeze.

Eggplants *See* **Aubergines**

Eggs
You can freeze raw eggs, whole or separated. Plain, cooked eggs don't freeze well. Do not freeze hard-boiled (hard-cooked) eggs.

To freeze
Whole: Freeze singly or in pairs. Break into small foil or plastic containers. Remove the air, seal, label and freeze.

STORAGE TIME: 6 months

Beaten: Beat in ones or twos, adding 1.5 ml/¼ tsp salt or sugar to stabilise the mixture. Make sure you note whether the mixture is sweet or savoury!

STORAGE TIME: 6 months

Egg whites: Place singly or in pairs in clean, small plastic containers with lids. Alternatively, you can use ice cube trays: freeze the whites in the trays, and once frozen, tip out of the trays into a polythene bag, remove the air, seal, label and return to the freezer. Note how many cubes make up a white so you'll know how many to remove when ready to use.

STORAGE TIME: 6 months

Egg yolks: Break up yolks and mix with a pinch of salt or sugar per yolk. Freeze in ice cube trays. One medium yolk will fill one cube. Tip into a polythene bag, remove the air, seal, label and return to the freezer.

STORAGE TIME: 6 months

To thaw and use
Thaw in the fridge for several hours or at room temperature for 1–2 hours. Use as for fresh eggs.

Elderberries
Elderberry wine is probably one of the most popular home-brews in the UK. Elderberries also make a delicious jelly (clear conserve), fruit cordial, sorbet or sauce and are very good added to apples to flavour crumbles and pies or to serve with lamb or duck.

Select clusters of deep purple berries – if still red, they will be unripe and tasteless. Pick on a dry day, if possible.

To prepare
Rinse the bunches under cold, running water and pat dry on kitchen paper (paper towels). Strip the berries off the stalks using the prongs of a fork.

To freeze
Dry-freezing, unsweetened: Use this method if making into wine or jelly later. Spread the berries in a single layer on a baking (cookie) sheet. Open-freeze until firm. Tip into polythene bags or rigid containers. Remove the air, seal, label and freeze.

STORAGE TIME: 12 months

Dry-freezing, sweetened: Pack in layers in a rigid container, sprinkling sugar between each layer. Use about 100 g/4 oz/½ cup caster (superfine) sugar to each 450 g/1 lb fruit. Remove the air, seal, label and freeze.

STORAGE TIME: 12 months

Purée-freezing: Use this method if making into sauces. Put just enough cold water in a saucepan to cover the base. Add the berries and heat gently, stirring occasionally until the juices run, then simmer for 3–4 minutes until tender. Purée in a blender or food processor or rub through a sieve (strainer). Sweeten to taste. Tip into a rigid container, leaving 2.5 cm/1 in headspace. Remove the air, seal, label and freeze.

STORAGE TIME: 12 months

To thaw and serve
Thaw at room temperature for 2–3 hours, then use as required.

Enchiladas

To prepare
Make in your usual way but don't add cheese or salad stuffs.

To freeze
Individual rolls: Wrap separately in clingfilm (plastic wrap), then place in a polythene bag or rigid container. Remove the air, seal, label and freeze.

STORAGE TIME: 3 months

Ready to serve: Place 8 enchiladas in a foil-lined shallow dish. Sprinkle with grated cheese. Open-freeze until firm, remove the dish, wrap in foil, label and return to the freezer.

STORAGE TIME: 3 months

To thaw and serve

Individual rolls: Thaw in their wrappers. Unwrap, place in a shallow dish and cover with grated cheese. Reheat as below.

Ready to serve: Remove the wrappings and return the enchiladas to the shallow dish. Cover loosely with foil and thaw at room temperature for 2–3 hours or overnight in the fridge. Reheat in a hot oven at 200°C/400°F/gas mark 6 (fan oven 180°C) for 20–25 minutes until piping hot throughout. Alternatively, cover with clingfilm, rolled back at one edge, and microwave on Full Power for about 5–8 minutes until piping hot throughout.

f

Falafels

These are best frozen uncooked, ready to fry (sauté) before serving.

To prepare
Make in your usual way and shape into small cakes.

To freeze
Place on non-stick baking parchment on a baking (cookie) sheet and open-freeze until firm. Pack in polythene bags or a rigid container. Remove the air, seal, label and freeze.
STORAGE TIME: 6 months

To thaw and serve
Arrange in a single layer on non-stick baking parchment on a baking sheet. Cover loosely with paper or foil and thaw at room temperature for 2 hours. Fry in hot oil until golden on both sides. Drain on kitchen paper (paper towels) and serve hot.

Fast-freeze facility

The 'fast freeze' switch overrides the thermostat so the temperature drops to between –23°C and – 30°C/–13°F and – 22°F, freezing food much more quickly. This is essential if you are freezing large quantities of food in one go. For more details, see Freezing Principles, page 23.

Fava beans   See **Beans, broad**

Fennel

Select firm white bulbs, with fresh, green feathery leaves. Avoid any that are limp or discoloured.

To prepare
Trim off the green fronds and chop finely. Scrape the outer white stalks, to remove the strings. Trim the base, then cut each head in quarters lengthways.

To freeze

Fronds: Place in a rigid container, remove the air, seal, label and freeze.
STORAGE TIME: 6 months
Heads: Blanch the quarters in boiling water for 3 minutes. Drain and plunge immediately in a bowl of iced water to cool. Drain again and dry on kitchen paper (paper towels). Pack in convenient quantities in polythene bags. Remove the air, seal, label and freeze.
STORAGE TIME: 6 months

To thaw and serve

Fronds: Use the chopped fronds from frozen as a herb. Add to soups, sauces and stuffings.
Heads: Cook the quartered heads from frozen in boiling, lightly salted water for 6 minutes or until just tender, and toss in butter. Alternatively, brush with olive oil and grill (broil) from frozen until golden and tender, or thaw slightly, cut into slices or matchsticks and use as part of a stir-fry.

Figs

Fresh figs freeze well – ideal if you have a tree in your garden. Select ripe fruit with undamaged skin.

To prepare

Wash each fruit individually and pat dry with kitchen paper (paper towels).

To freeze

Dry-freezing, unsweetened: Arrange on a baking (cookie) sheet and open-freeze until firm. Pack in polythene bags or rigid containers. Remove the air seal, label and return to the freezer.
STORAGE TIME: 12 months
Syrup-freezing: Make a light sugar syrup by dissolving 225 g/8 oz/1 cup granulated sugar in 600 ml/1 pt/2½ cups water in a saucepan. Poach the figs in the syrup for about 4–5 minutes until tender but still holding their shape. Cool quickly. Spoon the fruit in convenient quantities in rigid containers and pour the syrup over. Remove the air, seal, label and freeze.
STORAGE TIME: 12 months

To thaw and serve

Thaw at room temperature for 2–4 hours. Poached figs may be reheated and served hot, if liked.

Filo pastry (paste)

Filo pastry is a useful standby and can be bought fresh or ready-frozen.

To freeze

Place in its packaging in the freezer. The pastry damages easily, so take care not to squash the packaging.
STORAGE TIME: 6 months

To thaw and serve

Thaw in the fridge for 2–3 hours. Remove the number of sheets you need. Re-wrap and re-freeze any unused sheets immediately. Wrap the sheets you wish to use in clingfilm (plastic wrap) or a damp tea towel (dishcloth) until ready to use as required to prevent them from drying out.

Fish   *See individual entries, e.g.* **Cod, Salmon**

Fish cakes

Fish cakes are best frozen uncooked, ready for a quick meal.

To prepare

Make in your usual way.

To freeze

Place on non-stick baking parchment on a baking (cookie) sheet. Open-freeze until firm. Pack in polythene bags, remove the air, seal, label and return to the freezer.
STORAGE TIME: 2 months

To thaw and serve

Either defrost in the fridge for several hours or overnight or cook from frozen, adding 3–4 minutes' extra cooking time.

Fish fingers

Frozen fish fingers are a family friend. There is no point in making your own! Choose a good-quality brand that you know your family enjoy. Be wary of economy brands that are made with minced (ground) fish – they won't be pure fillet and can contain any part of the creature.

To thaw and serve

Grill (broil) or fry (sauté) from frozen, according to packet directions.

Flageolets   *See* **Beans, dried**

Flan cases, biscuit (cookie) base

A biscuit base makes a good standby in the freezer.

To prepare

Crush the biscuits and mix with melted butter in your usual way. Press into a foil, metal or porcelain flan dish (pie pan) or into a flan ring set on a slightly larger circle of non-stick baking parchment on a baking (cookie) sheet.

To freeze

Open-freeze until firm, then, if in a dish, wrap in polythene, remove the air, seal, label and return to the freezer. If in a ring, carefully remove the ring and transfer the flan case, with the help of the baking parchment, to a rigid container. Remove the air, seal, label and freeze.

STORAGE TIME: 6 months

To thaw and serve

Fill while still frozen. If serving hot, heat from frozen according to the chosen recipe (it will thaw in the time it takes to cook the filling). If serving cold, it will thaw while the filling is setting.

Flan cases, pastry (pie shells)

Flan cases are ideal to have in the freezer, ready to be filled when you need them. They can be frozen raw or cooked.

To prepare

Make the pastry (paste) in your usual way, roll out and use to line a metal, porcelain or foil flan dish (pie pan). Alternatively, line a flan ring set on a slightly larger circle of non-stick baking parchment on a baking (cookie) sheet. Prick the base with a fork. Either freeze raw, or bake in your usual way, then cool completely before freezing.

To freeze

In a dish: Place in a polythene bag, remove the air, seal, label and freeze.
STORAGE TIME: 6 months
In a flan ring: Open-freeze until firm, then carefully remove the ring and transfer to a rigid container, with the help of the baking parchment. Remove the air, seal, label and return to the freezer.
STORAGE TIME: 6 months

To thaw and serve
Raw: Cook from frozen in your usual way, then fill, or fill then cook.
Cooked: Thaw at room temperature for 1 hour, then fill and use as required.

See also **Flans, sponge** *and* **Shortcrust pastry**

Flan cases, sponge
Home-made sponge flan cases: These are well worth freezing, but take care as they will be very fragile.

To prepare
Make and bake in your usual way. Turn out on to a wire rack and leave to cool.

To freeze
Pack in rigid containers. Remove the air, seal, label and freeze.
STORAGE TIME: 6 months
Bought sponge flan cases: These are a useful standby. Freeze in their packaging.
STORAGE TIME: 6 months

To thaw and serve
Defrost at room temperature, fill and serve as required. For speed, they can be filled while still frozen, then thawed in the fridge until ready to serve.

Flans, pastry (paste) *See* **Quiches and gougères**

Flapjacks
Flapjacks can be frozen (a good idea if you find them hard to resist!)

To prepare
Make and cook in your usual way. Cool on a wire rack.

To freeze
Pack in a rigid container, interleaved with polythene interleave sheets, greaseproof (waxed) paper or non-stick baking parchment. Remove the air, seal, label and freeze.
STORAGE TIME: 6 months

To thaw and serve
Thaw at room temperature, then store in the rigid container.

Flat beans *See* **Beans, flat**

Flounders

Check with your fishmonger that the fish has not been previously frozen. Choose firm fish with a fresh smell. Avoid any that appears wet or slimy.

To prepare

Clean, if necessary. Trim the fins and tail and scrape off the scales. Cut the fish into halves, fillets or slices.

To freeze

Interleave with polythene interleave sheets or clingfilm (plastic wrap). Pack in polythene bags. Remove the air. Seal, label and freeze.

STORAGE TIME: 3 months

To thaw and serve

Thaw in the fridge, then cook in your usual way, or cook from frozen, allowing an extra 3–5 minutes' cooking time.

Flour tortillas *See* **Tortillas, flour**

Foil

Heavy-duty or freezer foil is ideal for wrapping foods to be frozen – especially those that are going to be reheated from frozen. It is also useful for protecting bone ends so they don't pierce the polythene bag they are wrapped in. Always make sure you wrap the foil tightly round the food to protect it fully. Foil containers with lids are also extremely useful for freezer-to-oven dishes.

Fondant icing (frosting)

Fondant or ready-to-roll icing can be frozen either on its own or on a cake. Make sure it is thoroughly wrapped to prevent moisture getting to it. Commercially prepared icing can be kept in its pack, unopened in the store cupboard for about the same time without hardening.

STORAGE TIME: 3 months

Frankfurters

Loose, vacuum-packed and canned frankfurters that have been opened can all be frozen.

To freeze

Pack loose ones in convenient quantities in polythene bags. Put canned ones with any remaining liquid in a rigid container. Remove the air, seal, label and freeze. Freeze vacuum packs as they are, but remember to label before freezing.
STORAGE TIME: 2 months

To thaw and serve

Cook from frozen, allowing an extra 3–5 minutes' cooking time until piping hot throughout. Alternatively, thaw in the fridge overnight, then cook in your usual way.

Free-flow

This is the term for foods that are frozen with each piece kept separate so they can be tipped or spooned out of their storage container in the desired quantity. The foods – such as soft fruits, peas, diced meat or grated cheese – are spread out on a baking (cookie) sheet, then open-frozen in the freezer until firm. They can then be tipped into polythene bags or rigid containers, sealed, labelled and stored in the freezer.

See also **Open-freezing**

Freezer burn

This is damage caused by dehydration, making foods dry and tough. You will see the greyish-white marks on the exposed surfaces of any foods that are kept too long – especially if they have been poorly wrapped. It is particularly noticeable on meat, fish and poultry.

Sweetened frozen fruit sometimes develops a greyish deposit. This is sucrose hydrate, not freezer burn, and is harmless. It disappears when the fruit is defrosted.

Freezer load

This is the amount of fresh food that can be frozen in the freezer at any one time within a period of 24 hours without raising the freezer temperature. It is usually about 10 per cent of the total capacity of the freezer.

French (green) beans *See* **Beans, French**

Frosting *See* **Icing**

Fruit

Freezing is the easiest and quickest way to preserve fruit. Most don't even need blanching. Ascorbic acid or lemon juice may be added to fruits that discolour, such as bananas, pears, peaches and apples. See individual entries for quantities. Fruit can be frozen in several ways.

Dry-freezing, unsweetened: Spread on a baking (cookie) sheet, open-freeze, then pack in polythene bags or rigid containers. Remove the air, seal, label and store in the freezer.

Dry-freezing, sweetened: Layer the fruit with caster (superfine) sugar in rigid containers, using about 100 g/4 oz/½ cup per 450 g/1 lb fruit. Remove the air, seal, label and freeze. It is important to use caster sugar as it will make its own syrup when the fruit is defrosted.

Syrup-freezing: Make a light syrup using 225 g/8 oz/1 cup granulated sugar to every 600 ml/1 pt/2½ cups water or a heavy syrup using 350 g/12 oz/1½ cups sugar to every 600 ml/1 pt/2½ cups water. This is sufficient for about 900 g/2 lb fruit. Pour over the raw prepared fruit in rigid containers, remove the air, seal, label and freeze. Use light syrup for sweet, delicate fruits, and heavy syrup for sharp, denser ones.

See also individual fruits, e.g. **Apples**

Fruit buns *See* **Currant buns**

Fruit crumbles *See* **Crumbles, fruit**

Fruit pies *See* **Pies**

Fudge

Fudge keeps well in an airtight container but if you make a large quantity it can be frozen for later use.

To prepare

Make in your usual way and cut into squares.

To freeze
Wrap individual squares in squares of clingfilm (plastic wrap), then in a polythene bag or rigid container, or pack in a rigid container, interleaved with polythene interleave sheets or non-stick baking parchment. Remove the air, seal, label and freeze.
STORAGE TIME: 6 months

To thaw and serve
Arrange on a serving dish and thaw in the fridge for several hours or overnight, or at room temperature for 2 hours.

Fudge icing (frosting)
Speciality icings, such as fudge icing, may be frozen, to be shaped or piped to decorate the cake when thawed. This prevents any fancy decoration being damaged in the freezer. Some cooked icings can go rather granular on thawing. If this happens, place in a bowl over pan of hot water briefly, or microwave for a few seconds only, and beat thoroughly. Cool quickly, then use as required.

To prepare
Make in your usual way.

To freeze
Pack in a rigid container, remove the air, seal, label and freeze.
STORAGE TIME: 3 months

To thaw and serve
Thaw at room temperature for 2–3 hours, then use as required.

Galia melon *See* **Melon**

Game

All varieties of game, both two- and four-legged, can be frozen when in season to enjoy at other times of the year.

See individual entries, e.g. **Pheasant, Hare, Venison**

Gammon

Gammon rashers, steaks or joints are only worth freezing if on special offer and you eat them fairly often because cured meat with a high fat content goes rancid quite quickly. Select the leanest meat you can find.

To freeze

If bought loose, wrap firmly in clingfilm (plastic wrap), then foil. Label and freeze. If vacuum-packed, freeze as it is.

STORAGE TIME: 2 months

To thaw and serve

Thaw overnight in the fridge if possible. Rashers (slices) can be defrosted in the microwave on Medium–low, peeling off the thawed ones as soon as possible. If you think a gammon joint may be salty, thaw it in a pan of cold water overnight, then throw away the water.

Cook in your usual way.

Garbanzos *See* **Chick peas**

Garlic

Don't freeze garlic cloves – they taste musty when thawed. Use garlic sparingly for flavouring dishes to be frozen, and don't keep for too long.

Garlic bread

Garlic bread can be frozen short-term for convenience.

To prepare
Prepare in your usual way but do not bake.

To freeze
Wrap tightly in foil and freeze.
STORAGE TIME: 1 month

To thaw and serve
Cook from frozen, adding an extra 5 minutes' cooking time.

Gateaux

Gateaux freeze well. If decorated, make sure they are in a rigid container with plenty of headspace so the top does not get damaged by the lid. Alternatively, freeze undecorated and put the finishing touches on before serving.

To prepare
Make in your usual way, cool, fill and decorate, if liked.

To freeze
Open-freeze until firm, then pack in a rigid container, remove the air, seal, label and freeze.
STORAGE TIME: 3 months

To thaw and serve
Thaw in the fridge overnight or at room temperature for about 3 hours.
   Cream and chocolate decorations can be frozen separately, then put in place before thawing.

   See also **Chocolate, Cream**

Giblets

Giblets should be frozen separately from birds, as they will keep for a shorter time – 3 months as opposed to 6 or 12 months for the bird itself. Boil in water with herbs or other flavourings for use as stock or a base for soup. If you don't intend to use the bird before the giblets' storage time is up, make into stock and freeze for use as gravy with the bird.

Glassware

Fine glass dishes are not suitable for freezing as foods expand as they freeze and may crack the glass. Heavy-duty glass screw-topped jars can be used to store foods such as breadcrumbs, and glass oven-to-tableware can be used to freeze made-up dishes. Ideally, line the dish with foil before cooking, so the food can be removed once it is frozen. The foil can then be removed and the food returned to the dish for reheating in the oven or microwave.

Globe artichokes *See* **Artichokes**

Goose

Most geese will weigh 2.75–5.5 kg/6–12 lb and will feed up to 8 people.

Do not stuff geese before freezing. Remember that giblets will not store for as long as the bird, so should be wrapped separately.

To prepare and freeze

Ready-frozen geese: These need no preparation. Simply place in the freezer in their wrapping.

STORAGE TIME: 6 months

Ready-prepared, fresh farmed geese: Wrap any bone ends in foil to protect them. Overwrap in foil or a stronger polythene bag, then remove the air, seal, label and freeze.

STORAGE TIME: 6 months

Fresh, undressed geese: The goose should be plucked, then hung for 3–4 days before drawing. To loosen the feathers, put the whole bird in a large bowl and pour boiling water over it. Leave for 15 minutes, then pluck it (be warned, it's a lengthy business). After hanging, draw the bird and remove the head and feet. Reserve the heart, gizzard, liver and neck for stock. Discard the remainder. Wrap the giblets separately as they don't keep as well as the goose. Rinse the bird under cold, running water and dry inside and out with kitchen paper (paper towels). Truss the bird, wrap the bone ends in foil, then wrap in a polythene bag. Put the bag of giblets in as well. Remove the air, seal, label and freeze.

STORAGE TIME: Birds 6 months, giblets 3 months

To thaw and serve

Thaw at room temperature about 12 hours, depending on the size, or in the fridge for 24 – 36 hours. Prepare and cook in your usual way.

Gooseberries

Choose plump, even-sized fruit.

To prepare

Top and tail, wash and pat dry on kitchen paper (paper towels).

To freeze

Dry-freezing, unsweetened: Pack in convenient quantities in polythene bags or rigid containers. Remove the air, seal, label and freeze.

STORAGE TIME: 12 months

Purée-freezing: Stew as below but until the fruit is pulpy. Purée in a blender or food processor or pass through a sieve (strainer). Pack in convenient quantities in rigid containers, leaving 2.5 cm/1 in headspace. Remove the air, seal, label and freeze.

STORAGE TIME: 12 months

Stew-freezing: Put enough water in a saucepan to just cover the base. Add the gooseberries together with 100–175 g/4–6 oz/½–¾ cup granulated sugar for every 450 g/1 lb fruit. Cover and cook gently until the fruit is tender but still holds its shape. Cool, then pack in rigid containers. Remove the air, seal, label and freeze.

STORAGE TIME: 12 months

Syrup-freezing: Make a heavy syrup with 350 g/12 oz/1½ cups sugar to every 600 ml/1 pt/2½ cups water. Pack the fruit in convenient quantities in rigid containers. Pour over just enough syrup to cover the fruit, leaving 2.5 cm/1 in headspace. Remove the air, seal, label and freeze.

STORAGE TIME: 12 months

To thaw and serve

Thaw overnight in the fridge or for 2–3 hours at room temperature, then use as required. Stewed gooseberries can be heated from frozen either in a saucepan or in the microwave. Break up the block as soon as possible and stir gently and frequently.

Gougères *See* **Quiches and gougères**

Grapefruit

Select fresh-smelling fruit that feel heavy for their size.

To prepare

Halve and squeeze the juice, or peel, remove the pith and separate into segments.

To freeze

Juice: Pour into ice cube trays. Freeze, then tip into polythene bags. Remove the air, seal, label and freeze.

STORAGE TIME: 12 months

Dry-freezing, sweetened – segments: Pack the segments in convenient quantities in rigid containers, layering with caster (superfine) sugar, using about 225 g/8 oz/1 cup sugar for every 450 g/1 lb fruit.

STORAGE TIME: 12 months

To thaw and serve

Juice cubes: Put in glasses or a jug and thaw in the fridge overnight or at room temperature for 1–2 hours.

Segments: Thaw in the container at room temperature for 2–3 hours.

Grapes

Select plump, sweet fruit. Avoid any that are discolouring round the stalk end.

To prepare

Pull off the stalks. Halve and remove any pips. Leave seedless varieties whole.

To freeze

Syrup-freezing: Make a light syrup using 225 g/8 oz/1 cup granulated sugar for every 600 ml/1 pt/2½ cups water. Pack the fruit in convenient quantities in rigid containers. Pour just enough syrup over to cover the fruit, leaving 2.5 cm/1 in headspace. Remove the air, seal, label and freeze.

STORAGE TIME: 12 months

To thaw and serve

Thaw in the fridge overnight or at room temperature for 2–3 hours.

Gratin dishes

Vegetables that are cooked au gratin (with a cheese and breadcrumb crust) freeze well. Place the vegetables – such as broccoli, cauliflower, chicory or spinach – in a foil-lined serving dish, then coat in a cheese sauce and sprinkle with a little extra cheese and breadcrumbs or crushed cornflakes. Open-freeze until firm, then remove the dish. Wrap in foil, then a polythene bag, remove the air, seal, label and return to the freezer.

STORAGE TIME: 6 months

To thaw and serve

Remove the wrappers. Return to the original dish. Thaw at room temperature for 3–4 hours, then bake in a preheated oven at 190°C/375°F/gas mark 5 (fan oven 170°C) for 35–40 minutes until golden and hot through.

Gravy

Freeze leftover gravy from the Sunday roast – it is ideal for moistening and flavouring meat dishes. Note on the label which type of meat gravy it is. It can also be poured over sliced roast meat to keep it moist when frozen.

To freeze

Pour into ice cube trays. Freeze until firm, then tip into polythene bags, remove the air, seal, label and return to the freezer.

STORAGE TIME: 3 months

To thaw and serve

Each cube will give about 15 ml/1 tbsp liquid. Add frozen to meat dishes while cooking, or thaw at room temperature for about 1 hour, or melt in a saucepan or in the microwave and use as required.

Greaseproof (waxed) paper

Greaseproof paper cannot be used on its own to wrap foods in the freezer. It will become wet and won't protect the food. It can, however, be used as an inner wrapping or for layering before sealing in foil, polythene bags or rigid containers. I prefer to use non-stick baking parchment as it is tougher.

Green beans   See **Beans, French**

Green lentils   See **Lentils**

Greengages

Select ripe, unblemished fruit.

To prepare
Wash, halve and remove the stones (pits) or leave whole, if preferred.

To freeze
Dry-freezing, sweetened: Pack in layers in convenient quantities, sprinkling caster (superfine) sugar between each layer. (Use about 225 g/ 8 oz/1 cup sugar per 450 g/1b fruit.) Remove the air, seal, label and freeze.
STORAGE TIME: 12 months

Syrup-freezing: Make a heavy syrup using 350 g/12 oz/1½ cups granulated sugar to every 600 ml/1 pt/2½ cups water. Pack the damsons in convenient quantities in rigid containers, leaving 2.5 cm/1 in headspace. Pour just enough syrup over to cover the fruit. Remove the air, seal, label and freeze.
STORAGE TIME: 12 months

Purée-freezing: Put just enough water in a saucepan to cover the base. Add the stoned (pitted) fruit, cover and cook gently until the fruit is tender, stirring occasionally. Purée in a blender or food processor or pass through a fine sieve (strainer) and sweeten to taste. Pour in convenient quantities into rigid containers, leaving 2.5 cm/1 in headspace. Remove the air, seal, label and freeze.
STORAGE TIME: 12 months

To thaw and serve
Thaw at room temperature for about 3 hours, then use as required.

Grey mullet See **Mullet**

Ground meat See **Minced meat** *and individual meats, e.g.* **Beef**

Grouse

Grouse is a highly prized game bird and definitely worth freezing. The season is from August to December.

Select plump, fresh unprepared birds from a reliable supplier. Small birds will serve one person and should be roasted. Larger birds will serve 2–3 and should be casseroled.

To prepare and freeze

Hang for 3 days, then pluck and draw, removing the head and feet. Keep the neck, heart, gizzard and liver and discard the remaining entrails. Pack the giblets in a small polythene bag. Rinse the bird with cold water and dry inside and out with kitchen paper (paper towels). Truss.

Protect the bone ends with foil, then pack individually in polythene bags, with their bag of giblets. Remove the air, seal, label and freeze.

STORAGE TIME: Birds 6 months, giblets 3 months

To thaw and serve

Thaw in the fridge overnight, then roast or casserole in your usual way.

Guavas

Select firm fruit with shiny skins. Avoid any that are bruised or damaged. The colour may be white, yellow or red. It is not an indication of ripeness.

To prepare

Peel, halve and scoop out the seeds. Slice or dice.

To freeze

Dry-freezing, sweetened: Put the fruit in rigid containers, layering it with caster (superfine) sugar. Allow about 100–175 g/4 –6 oz/½ –¾ cup sugar per 450 g/1 lb fruit. Remove the air, seal, label and freeze.

STORAGE TIME: 12 months

Purée-freezing: Put just enough water in a saucepan to cover the base. Add the prepared guava, cover and cook gently until the fruit is soft. Purée in a blender or food processor, sweetening to taste with caster sugar. Pour in convenient quantities into rigid containers, leaving 2.5 cm/1 in headspace. Remove the air, seal, label and freeze.

STORAGE TIME: 12 months

Syrup-freezing: Make a light syrup, using 225 g/8 oz/1 cup granulated sugar for every 600 ml/1 pt/2½ cups water. Pack the fruit in convenient quantities in rigid containers. Pour over just enough syrup to cover the fruit, allowing 2.5 cm/1 in headspace. Remove the air, seal, label and freeze.

STORAGE TIME: 12 months

To thaw and serve

Thaw at room temperature for 3–4 hours, then use as required. Syrup-packed fruit can be heated from frozen, then simmered for 3–4 minutes.

Guinea fowl

Guinea fowl are now farmed like chicken and can be used in exactly the same way. Small ones are prepared like poussins (Cornish hens). Select plump birds with firm, creamy-white flesh.

To prepare and freeze

Ready-prepared, frozen: Birds bought like this from the supermarket may be frozen as they are.

STORAGE TIME: 6 months

Ready-prepared, fresh: Protect the bone ends with foil, then wrap in a polythene bag. Put the giblets in a separate small polythene bag inside the bird's bag. Remove the air, seal, label and freeze.

STORAGE TIME: 6 months

Fresh, undressed: Hang the bird for 3 days to tenderise it, then pluck and draw the bird. Keep the neck, gizzard, heart and liver and discard the remaining entrails. Place the giblets in a small polythene bag. Wash the bird inside and out with cold water and pat dry with kitchen paper (paper towels). Truss, wrap bone ends in foil, then overwrap with a polythene bag. Place in a larger bag, together with the bag of giblets. Remove the air, seal, label and freeze.

STORAGE TIME: Birds 6 months, giblets 3 months

To thaw and serve

Thaw overnight in the fridge; as soon as totally defrosted, cook in your usual way.

h

Haddock

Check with your fishmonger that the fish has not been frozen before. The flesh should be firm and white with a fresh smell. If whole, the eyes and gills should be bright.

To prepare
Clean whole fish, remove the head and tail and then fillet. Cut fillets into useable portions, if necessary. Rinse with cold water and pat dry on kitchen paper (paper towels).

To freeze
Interleave fillets with polythene interleave sheets or clingfilm (plastic wrap), then pack in polythene bags, remove the air, seal, label and freeze.
STORAGE TIME: 3 months

To thaw and serve
Thaw at room temperature for 2 hours, separating the fillets as soon as possible, then cook in your usual way. Alternatively, cook from frozen, allowing 3–5 minutes' extra cooking time.

Haddock, smoked

Select fish with moist, not wet, flesh. Avoid any that is drying at the thinner, tail end. If dyed, the colour should be bright (I prefer the undyed variety, which are a pale, creamy colour rather than bright yellow).

To prepare
Cut the fish into portion sizes.

To freeze
Interleave with polythene interleave sheets or clingfilm (plastic wrap) and pack in polythene bags. Remove the air, seal, label and freeze.
STORAGE TIME: 3 months

To thaw and serve
Poach in milk or water from frozen, allowing 3–5 minutes' extra cooking time.

Hake

Check with your fishmonger that the fish has not been frozen before. The flesh should be firm and white with a fresh smell.

To prepare
Clean whole fish, remove the head and tail and then fillet. Cut the fish into useable portions of fillet or steaks, if necessary. Rinse with cold water and pat dry on kitchen paper (paper towels).

To freeze
Interleave fillets or steaks with polythene interleave sheets or clingfilm (plastic wrap), then pack in polythene bags, remove the air, seal, label and freeze.
STORAGE TIME: 3 months

To thaw and serve
Thaw at room temperature for 2 hours, separating fillets as soon as possible, then cook in your usual way. Alternatively, cook from frozen, allowing 3–5 minutes' extra cooking time.

Halibut

Halibut doesn't freeze as well as some fish as it tends to dry out when cooked after freezing. To help prevent this, freeze for a short time only, cook from frozen and serve with a sauce.

Check with your fishmonger that the fish has not been previously frozen. Smaller halibut (known as chicken halibut) are sold whole and will serve 4–6 people. Larger fish are sold filleted.

Choose firm fish with a fresh smell. Avoid any that appears wet or slimy.

To prepare
Clean, if necessary. Trim the fins and tail and scrape off the scales. Cut the fish into halves, fillets or slices.

To freeze
Interleave with polythene interleave sheets or clingfilm (plastic wrap). Pack in polythene bags. Remove the air. Seal, label and freeze.
STORAGE TIME: 6 weeks

To thaw and serve
Cook from frozen, allowing an extra 3–5 minutes' cooking time.

Halloumi cheese *See* **Cheese, hard**

Ham, cooked

Ready-cooked, sliced ham does not freeze well because of its high salt and water content. It may, however, be frozen in sandwiches. It is also possible to freeze ham pieces to use in cooked dishes.

To prepare
Remove any excess fat and cut into even-sized dice.

To freeze
Pack in convenient quantities in polythene bags. Remove the air, seal, label and freeze.

STORAGE TIME: 1 month

To thaw and serve
Thaw at room temperature for 2–3 hours or in the fridge overnight to add to dishes during cooking. Can be cooked from frozen.

Ham, raw, cured

These hams, such as Parma, Serrano and Westphalian, can all be frozen for a short time. It is not worth freezing vacuum-packed ham, as the shelf-life when stored in the fridge will be much the same. Select the leanest slices you can find as the fat will go rancid quickly.

To prepare
Make sure the slices are already interleaved; if not, do this with non-stick baking parchment. Wrap flat in a polythene bag. Remove the air, seal, label and freeze.

STORAGE TIME: 1 month

To thaw and serve
Thaw in the fridge overnight and use as required.

Hamburgers   *See* **Burgers**

Hare

Hare is classed as game and is available from August to March.

To choose

Large hares need long, slow cooking – called jugging – so if you are planning to roast it, choose a small, young one. Jugged hare is ideal for the freezer as the flavour improves when cooked, then reheated.

To prepare

Clean the hare but leave on its fur, then hang it for 4–5 days. Skin and cut into portions or halve if smaller. Rinse with cold water and pat dry on kitchen paper (paper towels).

To freeze

Raw: Wrap in foil to protect the bone ends, then place in a polythene bag, remove the air, seal, label and freeze.

STORAGE TIME: 6 months

Cooked: Jug the hare in your usual way. Cool quickly. Line a casserole dish (Dutch oven) with foil, then add the cold, cooked food. Open-freeze until firm. Remove the dish. Overwrap the block of casseroled food in more foil or place in a polythene bag. Remove the air, seal, label and freeze.

STORAGE TIME: 3 months

To thaw and serve

Raw: Thaw in the fridge overnight or at room temperature for several hours, then cook in your usual way.

Cooked: Remove all wrapping and put the jugged hare back in the casserole dish. Thaw at room temperature for 4–5 hours or in the microwave on Medium–low for 15–20 minutes, stirring frequently. Reheat in a preheated oven at 180°C/350°F/gas mark 4 (fan oven 160°C) for about 45 minutes until piping hot. Alternatively, heat in the microwave for about 15 minutes on Full Power, stirring occasionally, until piping hot throughout.

Haricot (navy) beans *See* **Beans, dried**

Headspace

This is the gap between the top of liquid or semi-liquid foods and the rim of the rigid container they are being frozen in. It is important to leave this gap as liquids expand by about 10 per cent when frozen. The usual headspace is about 2.5 cm/1 in.

You should also leave headspace above soft items such as icing (frosting) on cakes so that they do not become damaged by contact with the covering.

Herb bread

Herb bread freezes well for short periods.

To prepare
Prepare in your usual way but do not bake.

To freeze
Wrap tightly in foil and freeze.
STORAGE TIME: 1 month

To thaw and serve
Cook from frozen, adding an extra 5 minutes' cooking time.

Herbs

Fresh herbs freeze well and are convenient for cooking but they are not suitable for garnishing as they will appear wet and limp when thawed.

To prepare and freeze
Pre-packed herbs: These require no preparation.
STORAGE TIME: 6 months
Freshly picked herbs: Strip the leaves from any woody stalks, like rosemary, sage or thyme. This is not necessary with fleshy stalks, like parsley or coriander (cilantro), which have a lot of flavour in their stalks. Finely chop – the easiest way is to put them in a cup and snip them with scissors. Alternatively, leave sprigs whole.

Pack chopped herbs in small rigid containers or screw-topped jars. Put sprigs in polythene bags. Remove the air, seal, label and freeze.
STORAGE TIME: 6 months

To thaw and use
Use from frozen. Ready-chopped herbs can be spooned out of the container as required. Sprigs can be chopped while still frozen and used immediately.

Herrings

Herrings are cheap, nutritious and very underrated. Check with your fishmonger that they have not been previously frozen. Select very fresh fish with bright eyes and gills and a pleasant smell.

To prepare
Clean, scale and leave whole, or remove the heads, fins and tails, split open and bone. Rinse with cold water and pat dry on kitchen paper (paper towels).

To freeze
'Close' fish that have been split and boned. Wrap each fish individually in clingfilm (plastic wrap), then place in a polythene bag. Remove the air, seal, label and freeze.
STORAGE TIME: 2 months

To thaw and serve
Thaw just enough so that you can make several slashes on either side of whole fish; open out boned fish. Cook in your usual way, allowing an extra 3–5 minutes' cooking time.

Herrings, soused

To prepare
Prepare and cook in your usual way, then cool quickly in the liquid.

To freeze
Pack the rolled fish in a rigid container and pour the strained liquid over. Remove the air, seal, label and freeze.
STORAGE TIME: 1 month

To thaw and serve
Thaw in the fridge overnight. Drain and serve.

Hollandaise sauce
This is not suitable for freezing as the egg will curdle on thawing.

Honeydew melon   *See* **Melon**

Horseradish

Some people freeze horseradish already dressed with cream. I find it keeps better frozen without the cream, which can be added on thawing. Serve with roast beef, smoked mackerel or other dishes or use for flavouring stuffings, casseroles and stir-fries. Use young roots – old ones will be woody and unpalatable.

To prepare
Wash, peel and grate. Mix with 10 ml/2 tsp lemon juice per 30 ml/2 tbsp grated horseradish.

To freeze
Pack in ice cube trays. Freeze until firm, then tip into a polythene bag, remove the air, seal, label and return to the freezer.
STORAGE TIME: 6 months

To thaw and serve
Remove as many cubes as you need. Defrost at room temperature for about 1 hour. Mix with double cream, sugar and vinegar to taste for a sauce or use as required for flavouring.

Hot cross buns

To freeze
Place in polythene bags, remove the air, seal, label and freeze.
STORAGE TIME: 4 months

To thaw and serve
Thaw at room temperature in their bags for 2 hours or thaw in the microwave on Medium–low for a few seconds per bun, then reheat for a few seconds per bun on Full Power. Alternatively, wrap in foil and bake in a hot oven at 200°C/400°F/gas mark 6 (fan oven 180°C) for 5–10 minutes until thawed and warm. If you have a serrated-edged knife, you can halve them while frozen and toast.

Hot dog sausages

Loose, vacuum-packed and leftover canned hot dog sausages can be frozen.

To freeze

Loose: Pack in convenient quantities in polythene bags. Remove the air, seal, label and freeze.

STORAGE TIME: 2 months

Vacuum-packed: Freeze the pack as it is but remember to label it.

STORAGE TIME: 2 months

Leftover canned: Put with any remaining liquid in a rigid container. Remove the air, seal, label and freeze.

STORAGE TIME: 2 months

To thaw and serve

Cook from frozen, allowing an extra 3–5 minutes' cooking time, until piping hot throughout. Alternatively, thaw in the fridge overnight, then cook in your usual way.

Hot dogs, in buns

Hot dogs can be frozen in buns.

To prepare

Split the finger rolls and add a cold hot dog sausage to each. Wrap individually, tightly in foil, if reheating in the oven, or clingfilm (plastic wrap) if reheating in the microwave, then pack in a polythene bag. Remove the air, seal, label and freeze.

STORAGE TIME: 2 months

To thaw and serve

Thaw in the fridge overnight or at room temperature for about 2 hours. If foil-wrapped, heat in a moderate oven at 180°C/350°F/gas mark 4 (fan oven 160°C) for about 15 minutes. If in clingfilm, pierce the film in several places and heat in the microwave on Full Power for 1–3 minutes for 4 rolls, depending on the output of your oven.

Hummus

Hummus has a high garlic and oil content, so does not freeze well.

Huss

Huss, or rock salmon, has firm pinkish flesh and a single thick backbone down the centre. It should look moist and smell pleasant. Check with your fishmonger that it has not been previously frozen.

To prepare
Cut into individual portions, if necessary.

To freeze
Wrap individually in clingfilm (plastic wrap), then in a polythene bag. Remove the air, seal, label and freeze.

STORAGE TIME: 3 months

To thaw and serve
Cook from frozen in your usual way, allowing an extra 3–5 minutes' cooking time. Alternatively, thaw at room temperature for 2–3 hours and cook as soon as possible.

I

Ice cream

To freeze

Commercially prepared ice creams: These should be transferred to the freezer as soon as possible after buying as they must not be allowed to defrost even partially. NEVER re-freeze thawed ice cream.

STORAGE TIME: 3 months, unless otherwise stated on the packaging

Home-made ice cream: Follow your usual recipe. The secret of home-made ice cream is to break up the ice crystals thoroughly. It is vital to whisk the mixture with a fork during the freezing process so it becomes fluffy and light. It is worth buying an ice cream churn if you make it frequently.

STORAGE TIME: 3 months

To thaw and serve

Commercially prepared: Serve straight from the freezer unless otherwise directed.

Home-made: Remove from the freezer 10–15 minutes before serving to soften slightly.

Ice crystals

Ice crystals are formed when the moisture in food freezes. The faster food is frozen, the smaller the crystals, and the better the food will be preserved.

The ice crystals, or frost, that accumulates inside the freezer cabinet should be removed as soon as the layer is about 5 mm/¼ in thick. If not, it may impair the efficiency of the freezer.

See also **Defrosting**

Iceberg lettuce *See* **Lettuce**

Icing (frosting) *See individual entries, e.g.* **Fondant icing**

Interleaves

These are polythene sheets to use for separating slices or individual layers of food so they don't stick together. You can use clingfilm (plastic wrap), non-stick baking parchment or foil instead.

J

Jam (conserve)

There is no need to freeze ordinary jam as it keeps for months in a jar.

You can make uncooked freezer jam, which is much quicker to make than boiled jam and brings out the true flavour of the fruit. The minimum you can make uses 225 g/8 oz fruit.

To prepare

Select 225 g/8 oz soft, ripe fruit such as raspberries, strawberries, apricots, greengages, cherries, plums, peaches or nectarines.

Skin the fruits, if appropriate. Halve and remove any stones (pits), if necessary. Crush the fruit with a wooden spoon or fork or partially purée in a blender or food processor. Don't reduce to a liquid as you still want some 'bits' in your jam. Add 7.5 ml/1½ tsp lemon juice and 450 g/1 lb/2 cups caster (superfine) sugar. Stir well until the sugar has dissolved, then leave to stand for 1 hour. Stir in 60 ml/4 tbsp liquid pectin.

To freeze

Spoon into small rigid containers, leaving 2.5 cm/1 in headspace. Remove the air, seal and label. Chill for 24–36 hours until set, then freeze.

STORAGE TIME: 12 months

To thaw and serve

Thaw in the fridge overnight before use. Store any remainder in the fridge and use within a week.

Tip: If using frozen fruit to make boiled jam, the pectin content may be reduced. To test this, put a small spoonful of the cooked, unsweetened fruit pulp in a glass and leave to cool. Add 15 ml/1 tbsp methylated spirit and shake gently. If a large clot forms, the pectin content is sufficient. If there are several small clots, there is insufficient to give a set, so add 30 ml/2 tbsp lemon juice for every 1.8 kg/4 lb fruit or liquid pectin according to the manufacturer's instructions.

Jam sponges   See **Cakes, sponge**

Jam tarts *See* **Tarts**

Jello *See* **Jelly**

Jelly (jello)

Your freezer can help set a jelly quickly but don't try to freeze jellies for later use. They will set but will go cloudy and look unappetising on thawing.

Jelly rolls *See* **Swiss rolls**

Jerusalem artichokes *See* **Artichokes**

Juices

Fruit juices in cartons or plastic bottles from the chiller cabinet of the supermarket can be frozen for a longer shelf life, and you can freeze freshly prepared juice.

To prepare and freeze

Fresh juices: Squeeze the juice from citrus fruits, or use a fruit press for apples, grapes or other juicy fruits. Either pour into ice cube trays and freeze until firm or pour in convenient quantities into screw-topped jars, leaving 2.5 cm/1 in headspace. Remove the air, seal, label and freeze.

STORAGE TIME: 12 months

Ready-made juices: Freeze in their carton or plastic bottle.

STORAGE TIME: 12 months

To thaw and serve

Thaw overnight in the fridge or at room temperature for 1–2 hours and use as fresh.

Jumbo shrimp *See* **Prawns**

Kale

Select dark green leaves, avoiding any with yellowing edges.

To prepare
Separate the leaves. Remove the thick stalks, wash well in cold water and drain.

To freeze
Blanch the whole leaves in boiling water for 1 minute. Drain and plunge immediately in a bowl of iced water to cool. Drain again, dry on kitchen paper (paper towels) and shred. Pack in convenient quantities in polythene bags. Remove the air, seal, label and freeze.
STORAGE TIME: 6 months

To thaw and serve
Cook from frozen in boiling, lightly salted water for 6–8 minutes.

Kebabs

Kebabs can be frozen, ready to cook at your leisure. Do make sure that the meat or fish has not been previously frozen. If you wish to store the kebabs in a rigid container, use soaked wooden skewers that will fit in the box. If you are using metal skewers, make sure you have a supply of corks.

To prepare
Marinate any meat or vegetables in your usual way and thread on wooden or metal skewers.

To freeze
Wooden skewers: Pack in a rigid container, interleaving the kebabs with polythene interleave sheets, clingfilm (plastic wrap) or non-stick baking parchment to keep them separate.
STORAGE TIME: 3 months
Metal skewers: Push a cork on the end of each one, then wrap individually in foil or clingfilm and place in a polythene bag. Remove the air, seal, label and freeze.
STORAGE TIME: 3 months

To thaw and serve

Defrost at room temperature for 2–3 hours, then grill (broil) in your usual way, brushing with a little oil. Alternatively, cook from frozen under a moderate grill (broiler), allowing an extra 5 minutes' cooking time, turning frequently and brushing with oil so the food does not burn.

Kidney beans, red or white *See* **Beans, dried**

Kidneys

All kidneys freeze well but they must be very fresh.

To prepare and freeze

Remove any skin and snip out the cores. Rinse with cold water and pat dry on kitchen paper (paper towels).

Lambs', pigs' or calves' kidneys: Leave whole or cut into halves. Wrap individually in clingfilm (plastic wrap), then place in a polythene bag. Remove the air, seal, label and freeze.

STORAGE TIME: 3 months

Ox (beef) kidney: Dice or slice. Put in convenient quantities in rigid containers or polythene bags. Remove the air, seal, label and freeze.

STORAGE TIME: 3 months

To thaw and serve

Thaw overnight in the fridge, then cook in your usual way.

King prawns (jumbo shrimp) *See* **Prawns**

Kippers

Fresh smoked kippers have the best flavour and are usually sold in pairs. Choose plump fish with moist flesh. Very brightly coloured fish have been heavily dyed and may be of dubious quality.

To freeze

Wrap individually in clingfilm (plastic wrap) and pack in polythene bags. Remove the air, seal, label and freeze.

STORAGE TIME: 3 months

To thaw and serve

Cook from frozen: either poach in milk or milk and water, or grill (broil), dotted with butter, adding an extra 3–5 minutes' cooking to your usual time.

Kitchen paper (paper towels)

Kitchen paper is useful for drying foods before freezing but is not suitable for wrapping them in the freezer.

Kiwi fruit

Kiwi fruit tend to go soft when thawed so are best frozen in syrup and then used as a base for a fruit salad.

To prepare

Peel off the skins and cut the fruit into slices.

To freeze

Syrup-freezing: Make a light sugar syrup, using 225 g/8 oz/1 cup granulated sugar for every 600 ml/1 pt/2½ cups water. Add 15 ml/1 tbsp lemon juice. Pack the fruit in convenient quantities in rigid containers. Pour just enough syrup over to cover. Remove the air, seal, label and freeze.
STORAGE TIME: 12 months

To thaw and serve

Thaw in the fridge overnight or at room temperature for 2–3 hours, then use as part of a fruit salad.

Kohlrabi

This unusual vegetable is similar to the turnip. Avoid the largest specimens, as they will be woody. Choose medium-sized ones with firm stalks.

To prepare

Cut off any stalks and leaves. Peel and cut into even-sized chunks.

To freeze

Blanch in boiling water for 2 minutes. Drain and plunge immediately in a bowl of iced water to cool. Drain again and dry on kitchen paper (paper towels). Pack in convenient quantities in polythene bags. Remove the air, seal, label and freeze.
STORAGE TIME: 12 months

To thaw and serve

Cook from frozen in boiling, lightly salted water for about 6 minutes until tender. Drain and serve in pieces or mash with a little butter, pepper and nutmeg.

Kumquats

These baby orange-like fruits freeze very well. Select firm, unblemished fruit.

To prepare

I like to leave them whole, but they can be sliced, if you prefer.

To freeze

Dry-freezing, unsweetened: Spread out on a baking (cookie) sheet. Open-freeze until firm. Pack in a polythene bag, remove the air, seal, label and freeze.

STORAGE TIME: 12 months

Dry-freezing, sweetened: Pack in rigid containers, layering with 175 g/ 6 oz/¾ cup caster (superfine) sugar per 450 g/1 lb fruit. Remove the air, seal, label and freeze.

STORAGE TIME: 12 months

Syrup-freezing: Make a light sugar syrup using 225 g/8 oz/1 cup granulated sugar to every 600 ml/1 pt/2½ cups water. Pack the fruit in convenient quantities in rigid containers. Pour in just enough syrup to cover the fruit. Remove the air, seal, label and freeze.

STORAGE TIME: 12 months

To thaw and serve

Thaw overnight in the fridge or at room temperature for 2–3 hours. Use as required.

Labelling

Labelling is vital when freezing food. The label for each item should show
* The type of food
* The quantity
* The date it was frozen (or a 'use-by' date)
* Any special instructions, e.g. flavourings or extra ingredients to be added on defrosting, or cooking time required.

See also page 9

Ladies' fingers *See* **Okra**

Lamb

The cheapest way to buy lamb for the freezer is to buy a whole or half animal. Your butcher will prepare the meat to your requirements – you may, for example, want the shoulder and leg whole or cut into two joints. You can have the best end of neck as a rack or cut into cutlets, and you may want the breast boned for stuffing and rolling or cut into ribs for barbecuing. Ask him to label the packs ready for the freezer.

If you buy New Zealand lamb, it will be already frozen but can still be cut to suit your needs.

Bear in mind, if you buy a large part of an animal, it will probably include some cuts you would not normally use – for example, scrag end of lamb, which is not a popular cut, but perfect for stews, and liver and kidneys, which are much less popular than they used to be.

Select lean lamb. If buying ready-frozen, look particularly to make sure this is so (I was caught out recently, buying a frozen shoulder on special offer – when it had thawed, I trimmed off nearly 250 g/9 oz of fat!)

To prepare and freeze

Ready-wrapped, all cuts: If the meat is in suitable freezer packages, freeze it as it is (but if unsure, overwrap in polythene bags) and label for easy recognition.

STORAGE TIME: 12 months

Fresh joints, chops, cutlets and steaks: Wrap any bone ends in foil for protection, then wrap joints in polythene bags. Wrap chops, etc. individually in clingfilm (plastic wrap) or foil for easier usage, then in a polythene bag. Remove the air, seal, label and freeze.
STORAGE TIME: 12 months
Fresh minced (ground) and diced meat: Pack in convenient quantities in polythene bags. Remove the air, seal, label and freeze.
STORAGE TIME: Cubes 8 months, mince 3 months

To thaw and serve
Joints: Thaw at room temperature for up to 8 hours, then cook as usual.
Chops, cutlets and steaks: Thaw first or cook from frozen, allowing an extra 5 minutes' cooking time.
Mince: Can be cooked from frozen in a saucepan or the microwave, but break up the lump as soon as possible and make sure all the grains are separate and no longer pink before adding any remaining ingredients.
Diced meat: Cubes can be thawed or browned from frozen before adding the remaining ingredients. Add on 10 minutes' extra cooking time.

See also **Casseroles, Curries** *and* **Meat, cooked**

Lard (shortening)
Lard can be frozen but there is little point as it keeps for so long in the fridge – unless you render your own from a home-reared pig!

To freeze
Leave in its wrapper, or if home-prepared, wrap in greaseproof (waxed) paper. Place in a polythene bag. Remove the air, seal, label and freeze.
STORAGE TIME: 6 months

To thaw
Thaw in the fridge overnight or at room temperature for 1 hour before use.

Lasagne
Lasagne may contain meat, fish, vegetables or seafood. All are suitable for freezing.

To prepare
Make and cook in your usual way, but line the dish with foil. Cool quickly.

To freeze

Open-freeze until firm. Remove the dish, and wrap in foil, then a polythene bag. Remove the air, seal, label and freeze.

STORAGE TIME: 3 months

To thaw and serve

Remove all the packaging and return to the dish. Reheat from frozen in a moderately hot oven at 190°C/375°F/gas mark 5 (fan oven 170°C) for about 1 hour, covering the top loosely with foil to prevent over-browning. Alternatively, defrost in the fridge overnight or at room temperature for 3–4 hours, then reheat as above for about 35–40 minutes. It may also be defrosted in the microwave on Medium–low for 10–15 minutes, then reheated on Medium for 10–20 minutes until piping hot throughout.

Leeks

Large leeks can be tough so select small or medium-sized ones.

To prepare

Trim the roots and tops and remove any damaged outer leaves. If planning to leave whole, split the green down to the white part and rinse thoroughly under cold, running water. Alternatively, cut into slices, then wash thoroughly to remove any grit.

To freeze

Blanch in boiling water for 2 minutes. Drain, then plunge immediately in a bowl of iced water to cool. Drain again and dry on kitchen paper (paper towels). Pack in convenient quantities in polythene bags. Remove the air, seal, label and freeze.

STORAGE TIME: 6 months

To thaw and serve

Cook from frozen in boiling, lightly salted water for 6–10 minutes until just tender. Slices can be stir-fried or cooked from frozen in casseroles and stews.

Leerdammer cheese *See* **Cheese, hard**

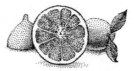

Lemon meringue pie

Commercially prepared pies freeze beautifully. Some home-made versions don't work so well and may become sticky when thawed. A pie that has been slow-baked to dry out the meringue will freeze better than one that has been 'flashed' in a hot oven.

To prepare
Make in your usual way.

To freeze
Place in a rigid container, deep enough to protect the meringue topping. Remove the air, seal, label and freeze.
STORAGE TIME: 1 month

To thaw and serve
Thaw in the fridge overnight. Serve cold.

Lemon sole   *See* **Sole**

Lemons

Lemons are a great cook's standby. You can often buy them in bulk much more cheaply than individually. If so, it's worth freezing the rind and juice.

To prepare
Grate or thinly pare off the rind from the lemons, then cut into halves and squeeze the juice.

To freeze
Rind: Put in a small rigid container, remove the air, seal, label and freeze.
STORAGE TIME: 12 months
Juice: Pour into an ice cube tray. Freeze, then tip into a polythene bag, remove the air, seal, label and return to the freezer.
STORAGE TIME: 12 months

To thaw and serve
Both rind and juice can be used from frozen for flavouring or garnishing hot dishes. Lemon juice can be thawed at room temperature for about 30 minutes before using, if liked.

Lentils

All dried lentils – brown, green, puy and red – will keep for many months uncooked in a store cupboard so they don't need to be frozen. But it's worth cooking a larger quantity of lentils than you need for one meal, then freezing the remainder for subsequent meals. Leftover canned lentils also be frozen.

To prepare
Dried: Soak, if necessary, and boil as usual, but without salt. Drain, rinse with cold water, then drain again and dry on kitchen paper (paper towels).
Leftover canned: No preparation is necessary.

To freeze
Dried, cooked: Pack in convenient quantities in polythene bags, remove the air, seal, label and freeze.
STORAGE TIME: 12 months
Leftover canned: Put into a rigid container, seal, label and freeze.
STORAGE TIME: 12 months

To thaw and serve
Thaw at room temperature, then use as required.

Lettuce

Lettuce cannot be frozen as a salad but the leaves may be made into a soup, which freezes well. The hearts can be frozen for use as a vegetable accompaniment or to be made into soup.

To prepare
Leaves: Remove the outer leaves of several heads of lettuce, wash and make into soup using your usual recipe, then cool quickly. Don't add any cream.
Hearts: Wash, then blanch the hearts in boiling water for 2 minutes. Drain. Plunge immediately in a bowl of iced water to cool. Drain again and dry on kitchen paper (paper towels).

To freeze
Soup: Pour into a rigid container, leaving 2.5 cm/1 in headspace. Remove the air, seal, label and freeze.
STORAGE TIME: 6 months
Hearts: Pack in convenient quantities in polythene bags. Remove the air, seal, label and freeze.
STORAGE TIME: 6 months

To thaw and serve
Soup: Reheat from frozen, then add any cream.
Hearts: Cook in boiling, lightly salted water for 2–3 minutes, then drain thoroughly and coat with a Hollandaise or cheese sauce. They can also be stir-fried from frozen for 4–5 minutes.

Lima beans   *See* **Beans, dried**

Limes
Lime zest and juice are very useful in cooking and worth freezing when you find bargains.

To prepare
Grate or thinly pare off the rind from the limes, then cut into halves and squeeze the juice.

To freeze
Rind: Put in a small rigid container, remove the air, seal, label and freeze.
STORAGE TIME: 12 months
Juice: Pour into an ice cube tray. Freeze, then tip into a polythene bag, remove the air, seal, label and return to the freezer.
STORAGE TIME: 12 months

To thaw and serve
Both rind and juice can be used from frozen for flavouring or garnishing hot dishes. Lime juice can be thawed at room temperature for about 30 minutes before using, if liked.

Lining containers
It's worth lining dishes with foil before cooking a dish like lasagne; you can also freeze a casserole in a straight-sided dish lined with foil. The containers can then be removed to save space in the freezer and to be used again. The foil can be removed and the food returned to the dish for reheating while still frozen.

When freezing liquids, line a straight-sided container with a polythene bag and then pour the liquid in. Once frozen, the container can be removed and the liquid will be a convenient shape to take up less space in the freezer. Remember to thaw the frozen bag of liquid in a receptacle as it will almost certainly leak.

Liver

Liver can be frozen if very fresh.

To prepare

Slice, rinse with cold water and pat dry on kitchen paper (paper towels).

To freeze

Interleave liver slices with polythene interleave sheets, clingfilm (plastic wrap) or non-stick baking parchment and pack in a polythene bag. Remove the air, seal, label and freeze.

STORAGE TIME: 3 months

To thaw and serve

Thaw overnight in the fridge, then cook in your usual way.

Liver pâté *See* **Pâtés**

Lobster

Lobsters must be very fresh to freeze.

To prepare

Either boil them yourself or buy ones that have just been cooked.

To freeze

Protect the pincers with foil, then wrap individually in clingfilm (plastic wrap) and overwrap in foil or a polythene bag. Remove the air, seal, label and freeze.

STORAGE TIME: 1 month

To thaw and serve

Thaw overnight in the fridge, then halve, remove the stomach sac from behind the head and the black vein that runs the length of the body and prepare in your usual way.

Loganberries

Select ripe but not mushy fruit. If over-ripe, they won't freeze well.

To prepare

Pick over and remove any stalks. Discard any damaged fruit.

To freeze

Dry-freezing, unsweetened: Spread out on a baking (cookie) sheet. Open-freeze until firm, then pack in polythene bags. Alternatively, pack directly in rigid containers. Remove the air, seal, label and freeze.

STORAGE TIME: 12 months

Dry-freezing, sweetened: Layer in rigid containers in convenient quantities with caster (superfine) sugar. Allow about 100 g/4 oz/½ cup sugar for every 450 g/1 lb fruit.

STORAGE TIME: 12 months

Purée-freezing: Purée the fruit in a blender or food processor, then pass through a sieve (strainer) to remove the seeds. Sweeten to taste, if liked, and spoon in convenient quantities into rigid containers, leaving 2.5 cm/1 in headspace. Remove the air, seal, label and freeze.

STORAGE TIME: 12 months

To thaw and serve

Dry-frozen: Thaw dry-frozen loganberries at room temperature for about 2 hours, then use as required, or add frozen if making a hot dish.

Purée: Thaw at room temperature before use or heat from frozen in a saucepan or in the microwave.

Loquats

Loquats, or Japanese medlars, are used mostly for jams (conserves) and jellies (clear conserves). A few slices may also be used to add a delicious bitter almond flavour to sauces and are particularly good with apricots or apples. For this reason you might like to freeze a few to add to these sauces when you make them. When buying, select even-sized conical fruits with unblemished skins.

To prepare

Wash and pat dry on kitchen paper (paper towels). Slice or leave whole.

To freeze

Slices: Spread slices out on a baking (cookie) sheet and freeze until firm. Pack in polythene bags. Remove the air, seal, label and freeze.
STORAGE TIME: 12 months
Whole fruit: Pack in polythene bags. Remove the air, seal, label and freeze.
STORAGE TIME: 12 months

To thaw and serve

Slices: Add to a sauce from frozen.
Whole fruit: Thaw whole ones at room temperature for 1 hour. Chop or slice, then add to apples or apricots before stewing for a sauce.

Low-fat spreads

Most reduced-fat spreads can be frozen. But the lower the fat content, the higher the water content, so the texture of the very low-fat ones may be impaired on thawing. Check individual labels for recommendations.

To freeze

Label unopened tubs with the date of freezing. Place as they are in the freezer.
STORAGE TIME: 3 months

To thaw and serve

Defrost overnight in the fridge, then use as fresh.

Lychees

Lychees have a wonderful flavour and I love to have a few to hand to add to a fruit salad or to serve with Parma ham for a change. Look for bargains when available. The casings should be a rich reddish-brown and firm. Avoid any that look dull or feel soft.

To prepare

Gently crack the outer casings with your nails and remove. Leave the stones (pits) in if dry-freezing, gently squeeze them out if freezing in syrup.

To freeze

Dry-freezing, unsweetened: Toss the fruit in a squeeze of lemon juice. Pack in rigid containers in convenient quantities. Remove the air, seal, label and freeze.
STORAGE TIME: 6 months

Syrup-freezing: Make a light syrup using 225 g/8 oz/1 cup granulated sugar and 15 ml/1 tbsp lemon juice for every 600 ml/1 pt/2½ cups water. Pack the fruit in convenient quantities in rigid containers. Pour over just enough syrup to cover the fruit, leaving 2.5 cm/1 in headspace. Remove the air, seal, label and freeze.

STORAGE TIME: 12 months

To thaw and serve
Thaw in the fridge overnight. Use as required.

m

Macaroni cheese

Macaroni cheese makes a useful standby supper.

To prepare and freeze

Cook the pasta and cheese sauce in your usual way and mix together. Line an ovenproof serving dish with foil and spoon in the mixture. When cold, cover with grated cheese. Open-freeze until firm, then remove the dish, wrap tightly in foil or in a polythene bag, remove the air, seal, label and freeze.

STORAGE TIME: 6 months

To thaw and serve

Remove the wrappings and return to the serving dish. Thaw overnight in the fridge or at room temperature for 3–4 hours. Cook in a moderately hot oven at 190°C/375°F/gas mark 5 (fan oven 170°C) for about 35 minutes until golden and piping hot. Alternatively, cook in the microwave on Full Power for about 6 minutes, then flash under a hot grill (broiler) to brown the top. Make sure it is piping hot throughout; if not, heat a little longer.

Mackerel

Mackerel are highly nutritious and inexpensive. Select very fresh fish with shiny skin, bright eyes and gills and a pleasant smell. Make sure that the fish have not been previously frozen.

To prepare

Clean and leave whole, or remove the heads, trim the fins and tails, split open and bone. Rinse with cold water and pat dry on kitchen paper (paper towels).

To freeze

'Close' fish that have been split open and boned. Wrap each fish individually in clingfilm (plastic wrap), then place in a polythene bag. Remove the air, seal, label and freeze.

STORAGE TIME: 2 months

To thaw and serve

Thaw whole fish just enough so that you can make several slashes on either side; open out boned fish. Cook in your usual way, allowing an extra 3–5 minutes' cooking time.

Mackerel, soused

To prepare

Prepare and cook in your usual way, then cool quickly in the liquid.

To freeze

Pack the rolled fish in a rigid container and pour the strained liquid over. Remove the air, seal, label and freeze.

STORAGE TIME: 1 month

To thaw and serve

Thaw in the fridge overnight. Drain and serve.

Mandarins

Mandarins are not as common now as clementines and satsumas so it's worth freezing them as their flavour is superior, in my opinion.

Select sweet-smelling fruit that have firm skins and feel heavy for their size. Those that are light or have loose skins may be dry.

To prepare

Peel, remove all the pith and segment. Remove any pips.

To freeze

Dry-freezing, sweetened: Pack in rigid containers in convenient quantities. Sprinkle each layer with 15–30 ml/1–2 tbsp granulated sugar. Remove the air, seal, label and freeze.

STORAGE TIME: 12 months

Syrup-freezing: Make a heavy sugar syrup using 350 g/12 oz/1½ cups granulated sugar to every 600 ml/1 pt/2½ cups water. Pack the segments in convenient quantities in rigid containers. Pour over the syrup to cover completely. Remove the air, seal, label and freeze.

STORAGE TIME: 12 months

To thaw and serve

Thaw at room temperature for 2–3 hours. Serve with breakfast cereals or ice cream, as part of a fruit salad or in a trifle.

Mangetout (snow peas)

Mangetout freeze well to be thawed and served as a vegetable accompaniment or as part of a stir-fry. Select crisp, bright green pods. Avoid any that look greyish or shrivelled.

To prepare
Top and tail. Blanch in boiling water for 1 minute. Drain and plunge in a bowl of iced water to cool. Drain again and dry on kitchen paper (paper towels).

To freeze
Spread out on a baking (cookie) sheet and open-freeze until firm, then pack in polythene bags. Alternatively, pack in convenient quantities in polythene bags. Remove the air, seal, label and freeze.
STORAGE TIME: 12 months

To thaw and serve
Cook from frozen in boiling, lightly salted water for about 3 minutes until just tender but still with some bite. May also be stir-fried from frozen.

Mangoes

Mangoes are becoming much more readily available these days. Look out for special offers and freeze them for delicious desserts. Select ripe mangoes that smell fragrant and give slightly when squeezed gently in the palm of your hand. Avoid any that are hard or very soft.

To prepare
Peel and cut all the flesh off the large, hairy stone (pit), then slice or dice.

To freeze
Syrup-freezing: Make a light sugar syrup using 225 g/8 oz/1 cup granulated sugar and 15 ml/1 tbsp lemon juice to every 600 ml/1 pt/2½ cups water. Pack the prepared fruit in convenient quantities in rigid containers. Pour just enough syrup over to cover, leaving 2.5 cm/1 in headspace. Remove the air, seal, label and freeze.
STORAGE TIME: 12 months

To thaw and serve
Thaw in the fridge overnight, then use as required.

Margarine

Margarine is hardly worth freezing, unless you want a back-up store.

To freeze
Blocks: Leave hard margarine in its wrapper, then wrap in foil. Seal, label and freeze.
STORAGE TIME: 3 months
Tubs: Tub margarine can be frozen unopened in its tub. Label with the date and freeze.
STORAGE TIME: 3 months

To thaw and use
Thaw in the fridge, then use as required.

Marinades

If you are mad about barbecues or grills, it's worth having some marinades ready made up for use. They do keep in the fridge for several weeks but can be frozen if required.

To prepare
Make in your usual way.

To freeze
Pour in convenient quantities in screw-topped jars or small rigid containers, leaving 2.5 cm/1 in headspace. Remove the air, seal, label and freeze.
STORAGE TIME: 6 months

To thaw and use
Defrost at room temperature for 1–2 hours or heat from frozen in a saucepan or in the microwave, then use as required.

Marjoram   *See* **Herbs**

Marlin

Marlin steaks can be frozen only if ready-frozen or freshly caught. Check with your fishmonger that it has not been previously frozen. Select even-sized thick steaks with moist flesh and a fresh smell.

To freeze

Wrap individually in clingfilm (plastic wrap), then in a polythene bag. Remove the air, seal, label and freeze.

STORAGE TIME: 3 months

To thaw and serve

Cook from frozen, allowing an extra 3–5 minutes' cooking time.

Marmalade

There is little or no point in freezing marmalade as it keeps unopened in the store cupboard for months. Opened jars should be kept in the fridge and used in about 3 weeks. However, Seville oranges can be frozen when in season to make into marmalade at other times of the year.

See also **Seville oranges**

Marrow (squash)

Marrows have a fairly short season, so it's worth freezing some for use at other times of the year. Select small or medium-sized marrows, depending on whether you want to stuff them or serve as a vegetable accompaniment.

To prepare

Peel if the skin is tough, then cut into rings or dice, as required. Blanch in boiling water for 2 minutes. Drain and place immediately in a bowl of iced water to cool. Drain again and dry on kitchen paper (paper towels).

To freeze

Pack in convenient quantities in polythene bags. Remove the air, seal, label and freeze.

STORAGE TIME: 12 months

To thaw and serve

To serve plain: Cook dice from frozen in boiling, lightly salted water for about 5 minutes until just tender. Drain thoroughly. Serve tossed in butter or in a sauce.

To stuff: Slices can be stuffed while still frozen, then baked in your usual way, allowing an extra 5–10 minutes' cooking time. Alternatively, thaw at room temperature for 1–2 hours, then stuff and cook in your usual way.

Marzipan

Marzipan does not need to be frozen. An unopened pack can be stored for months in the larder. If opened, put it in an airtight container and store it in the fridge.

Mayonnaise

Mayonnaise is not suitable for freezing: it will curdle once thawed and taste unpleasant.

Meat *See individual entries, e.g.* **Beef**

Meat, cooked

Leftover roast meat or poultry can be cut up and stored, preferably in gravy, for use another time.

To prepare
Carve into slices or cut into dice as appropriate.

To freeze
Place in convenient quantities in rigid containers. Cover with gravy (this will help keep it moist both in the freezer and when reheated). Leave 2.5 cm/1 in headspace. Remove the air, seal, label and freeze.
STORAGE TIME: 2 months

To thaw and serve
Thaw in the fridge overnight, then reheat in a saucepan, or cover and heat in a moderately hot oven at 190°C/375°F/gas mark 5 (fan oven 170°C). Alternatively, microwave on Medium. Make sure the meat is properly thawed and is piping hot throughout when reheated.

See also individual entries, e.g. **Ham, Salami, Meatballs**

Meat loaf

To prepare
Make in your usual way. Go easy on any flavouring, which may alter or intensify when thawed.

To freeze
Wrap the whole loaf in clingfilm (plastic wrap), or cut into slices and wrap individually, then overwrap tightly in foil. Label and freeze.
STORAGE TIME: 3 months

To thaw and serve
Thaw overnight in the fridge and serve cold or unwrap when frozen, remove the clingfilm, then re-wrap in foil, thaw, and heat through in a moderately hot oven at 190°C/375°F/gas mark 5 (fan oven 170°C) for about 30 minutes. Alternatively, unwrap, place in a microwave-safe dish, cover and reheat in the microwave on Full Power for about 1 minute per slice, 6 minutes if whole.

Meat pies

To prepare
Make and cook in your usual way.

To freeze
Wrap whole or individual pies in clingfilm (plastic wrap), then foil, or pack in a rigid container. Remove the air, seal, label and freeze.
STORAGE TIME: 3 months

To thaw and serve
They are best served hot. Thaw at room temperature for 2–5 hours, depending on the size and density of the pie. Cook in a moderately hot oven at 190°C/370°F/gas mark 5 (fan oven 170°C) for 20–45 minutes, depending on the size, covering the top loosely with foil if over-browning.

Meatballs
These can be frozen raw, or cooked in a sauce, then frozen.

To prepare
Make in your usual way, but remember, strong seasonings will intensify when thawed.

To freeze
Raw: Arrange on a baking (cookie) sheet. Open-freeze until firm, then pack in polythene bags, remove the air, seal, label and freeze.
STORAGE TIME: 3 months
Cooked: Cook the meatballs in your usual way. Place in convenient quantities in a rigid container and cover with sauce (e.g. tomato or barbecue), leaving 2.5 cm/1 in headspace. Remove the air, seal, label and freeze.
STORAGE TIME: 3 months

To thaw and serve
Raw: Cook raw meatballs from frozen, allowing an extra 2–3 minutes' cooking time.
Cooked: Thaw cooked balls in sauce in the fridge overnight, or at room temperature for 3–4 hours, or in the microwave on Medium–low. Reheat immediately on top of the stove, stirring gently and frequently, or in a moderately hot oven at 190°C/375°F/gas mark 5 (fan oven 170°C) for about 30 minutes, stirring once or twice until piping hot, or in the microwave for about 6 minutes on Full Power, stirring gently every minute.

Melon
Melon freezes well. Select fruit that give gently at one end when pressed.

To prepare
Halve, scoop out the seeds, then peel and cut into dice, or scoop the flesh out of the skin with a melon baller.

To freeze
Dry-freezing, sweetened: Pack in convenient quantities in rigid containers, layering with caster (superfine) sugar. Allow about 100 g/4 oz/ ½ cup sugar for every melon.
Syrup-freezing: Make a light syrup, using 225 g/8 oz/1 cup granulated sugar for every 600 ml/1 pt/2½ cups water. Pack the fruit in convenient quantities in rigid containers with just enough syrup to cover. Leave 2.5 cm/ 1 in headspace. Remove the air, seal, label and freeze.
STORAGE TIME: 6 months

To thaw and serve
Thaw in the fridge overnight. Use as required.

Meringues

Meringues freeze well. Pack carefully as they are very fragile.

To prepare

Make in your usual way – nests, shells, large rounds or pavlovas. Do not fill.

To freeze

Pack in rigid containers, lined with foil or non-stick baking parchment. Remove the air, seal, label and freeze.

STORAGE TIME: 12 months

To thaw and serve

They take only 5–10 minutes to thaw at room temperature, so fill and serve from frozen.

See also **Pavlovas**

Microwaving

A microwave oven is the perfect partner with the freezer. Use it to defrost foods (usually on Medium–low) and reheat foods from frozen (on Full Power or on Medium if defrosted first). See individual entries and follow your manufacturer's instructions.

When defrosting, you must thaw in short bursts so the food doesn't start to cook while thawing.

When reheating, make sure food is piping hot throughout. To test made-up dishes such as lasagne, stick a knife down through the centre and wait 5 seconds. The blade should now feel burning hot. If not, heat a little longer.

Milk

It's useful to freeze plastic or waxed cartons of milk for emergencies. Do not freeze bottles as they may crack as the liquid expands when frozen. Homogenised milk freezes best.

To freeze

Place in the sealed container in the freezer.

STORAGE TIME: 1 month

To thaw and serve

Milk takes ages to thaw. Stand the carton in a bowl of cold water in the fridge overnight. It's best not to leave it out at room temperature. Shake the milk well before opening as it will have separated when frozen.

Milk puddings

Milk puddings tend to become stodgy or look translucent when thawed. But it's probably better to freeze leftovers rather than waste them.

To prepare
Make and cook in your usual way.

To freeze
Tip into a rigid container, removing any skin. Pour enough milk over the surface to cover the top completely and leave 2.5 cm/1 in headspace. Remove the air, seal, label and freeze.

STORAGE TIME: 1 month

To thaw and serve
Thaw in the fridge overnight, then tip into a saucepan and heat gently, stirring frequently until hot through. Stir in a little more milk or, preferably, cream, if you like it creamy textured. Alternatively, place in a microwave-safe dish and heat on Full Power, stirring every minute until piping hot, adding a little more milk or cream, if necessary.

Mince pies

To prepare
Make in your usual way. Bake and cool on a wire rack.

To freeze
Pack in a polythene bag or rigid container. Remove the air, seal, label and freeze.

STORAGE TIME: 6 months

To thaw and serve
Place frozen on a baking (cookie) sheet. Bake in a hot oven at 220°C/425°F/gas mark 7 (fan oven 200°C) for about 15 minutes until hot through. Lay a sheet of foil loosely over the top if over-browning. Serve warm.

Minced (ground) meat

Choose good-quality, lean mince for freezing.

To freeze

Pack in convenient quantities in polythene bags. Remove the air, seal, label and freeze.

STORAGE TIME: 3 months

To thaw and serve

Mince can be cooked from frozen in a saucepan or microwave, but scrape off the outer meat as it browns, and break up the block as soon as possible. Keep cooking and stirring until all the grains are separate and no longer pink before adding any remaining ingredients.

See also individual entries, e.g. **Beef, Burgers**

Mint See **Herbs**

Mississippi mud pie

To prepare

Make in your usual way in a foil container or a foil-lined flan dish (pie pan). Cool. Do not decorate.

To freeze

In a foil container: Wrap in foil, label and freeze.

STORAGE TIME: 2–3 months

In a foil-lined dish: Open-freeze until firm. Remove the dish, wrap in foil or a polythene bag. Remove the air, seal, label and freeze.

STORAGE TIME: 2–3 months

To thaw and serve

Thaw overnight in the fridge. Decorate, if liked, before serving.

Moules à la marinière

To prepare
Prepare the mussels and cook in your usual way but avoid too much garlic. Cool quickly and remove any mussels that have not opened. To save space, snap off and discard the top shells, leaving the mussels in the bottoms.

To freeze
Tip in convenient quantities in rigid containers with all the liquid, allowing 2.5 cm/1 in headspace. Remove the air, seal, label and freeze.
STORAGE TIME: 1 month

To thaw and serve
Reheat from frozen in the cooking liquid until piping hot, Add lots of chopped fresh parsley.

Moussaka

To prepare
Make and cook in your usual way, using a foil-lined dish. Cool quickly.

To freeze
Open-freeze until firm. Remove the dish, wrap the moussaka in foil, then a polythene bag. Remove the air, seal, label and freeze.
STORAGE TIME: 3 months

To thaw and serve
Remove all the packaging and return to the dish. Reheat from frozen in a moderately hot oven at 190°C/375°F/gas mark 5 (fan oven 170°C) for about 1 hour, covering the top loosely with foil to prevent over-browning. Alternatively, defrost in the fridge overnight or at room temperature for 3–4 hours, then reheat as above for about 35–40 minutes, or defrost in the microwave on Medium–low for 10–15 minutes, then reheat on Medium for 10–20 minutes until piping hot throughout.

Mousses

Sweet and savoury mousses freeze well.

To prepare
Make in your usual way but do not decorate or garnish the top.

To freeze
Wrap in foil or a polythene bag. Remove the air, seal, label and freeze.
STORAGE TIME: 2 months

To thaw and serve
Defrost overnight in the fridge. Decorate or garnish according to whether sweet or savoury and serve cold.

Mulberries

Select ripe fruit that haven't gone mushy.

To prepare
Pick over and remove any stalks. Discard any damaged fruit.

To freeze
Dry-freezing, unsweetened: Spread out on a baking (cookie) sheet. Open-freeze until firm, then pack in polythene bags. Alternatively, pack directly in convenient quantities in rigid containers. Remove the air, seal, label and freeze.
STORAGE TIME: 12 months

Dry-freezing, sweetened: Layer in rigid containers in convenient quantities with caster (superfine) sugar. Allow about 100 g/4 oz/½ cup sugar for every 450 g/1 lb fruit. .
STORAGE TIME: 12 months

Purée-freezing: Purée the fruit in a blender or food processor, then pass through a sieve (strainer) to remove the seeds. Sweeten to taste, if liked, and spoon in convenient quantities into rigid containers, leaving 2.5 cm/1 in headspace. Remove the air, seal, label and freeze.
STORAGE TIME: 12 months

To thaw and serve
Dry-frozen: Thaw dry-frozen fruit at room temperature for about 2 hours, then use as required. They may be added frozen if making a hot dish.
Purée: Thaw at room temperature before use, or heat from frozen in a saucepan or in the microwave.

Mullet, red or grey

Mullet is suitable for freezing only if very fresh. Check that the fish hasn't been previously frozen. Select fish with a shiny skin, bright eyes and gills, and a fresh smell. Avoid any that look dull or have a strong smell.

To prepare

Clean and gut, if necessary. Remove the scales. Fillet the fish or leave whole, as preferred.

To freeze

Wrap fillets and whole fish individually in clingfilm (plastic wrap), then pack in a polythene bag. Remove the air, seal, label and freeze.

STORAGE TIME: 3 months

To thaw and serve

Thaw at room temperature for 2–3 hours, then cook as soon as possible. Alternatively, cook from frozen in your usual way, allowing an extra 3–5 minutes' cooking time.

Mung beans *See* **Beans, dried**

Mushrooms

All types of mushroom freeze well, either raw or cooked. Select very fresh mushrooms. Avoid any that are discoloured or shrivelling.

To prepare

Wipe with a damp cloth but do not wash. Trim, slice, if liked, or leave whole. Toss in 15 ml/1 tbsp lemon juice per 450 g/1 lb mushrooms to help prevent discolouring.

To freeze

Raw: Pack in convenient quantities in polythene bags. Remove the air, seal, label and freeze.

STORAGE TIME: 1 month

Fried (sautéed): Fry in a little butter or olive oil for 2 minutes. Cool quickly. Pack in convenient quantities in polythene bags or rigid containers. Remove the air, seal, label and freeze.

STORAGE TIME: 3 months

Stewed: Put just enough water in a saucepan to cover the base. Add the mushrooms, cover and cook gently for about 3 minutes until softened. Alternatively, cook in the same way in a bowl in the microwave. Cool quickly, turn into rigid containers in convenient quantities. Remove the air, seal, label and freeze.

STORAGE TIME: 3 months

To thaw and serve
Use from frozen in any dishes or reheat in a saucepan or in the microwave.

Mussels
Canned mussels can be frozen – useful if you need to use only half a can. Fresh ones should be frozen only if very fresh. Select fresh-smelling, closed shells with as few barnacles as possible. Avoid batches that have lots of broken or open shells.

To prepare
Canned: No preparation necessary. Put with their liquid in a rigid container.
Fresh: Scrub the shells under cold, running water, discarding any that are damaged or open and don't close when sharply tapped. Remove the beards. Steam in a little boiling water in a covered pan until the shells open, shaking the pan occasionally. Strain the cooking liquid into a rigid container. Remove the fish from the shells and add to the liquid. Cover and leave to cool.

To freeze
Canned and fresh: Lay a sheet of greaseproof (waxed) paper over the liquid to protect the fish. Remove the air, seal, label and freeze.

STORAGE TIME: 1 month

To thaw and serve
Reheat from frozen in the cooking liquid, seasoning to taste. Strain and serve in a sauce or in a pasta or rice dish or cooled and dressed in French dressing.

Mutton *See* **Lamb**

ŋ

Naan bread

All speciality breads freeze well.

To freeze

Vacuum-packed: No more preparation is necessary.
Loose and home-made: Wrap individually in polythene bags. Remove the air, seal, label and freeze.

STORAGE TIME: 6 months

To thaw and serve

Reheat from frozen either under the grill (broiler), or wrapped in foil in a preheated oven at 200°C/400°F/gas mark 6 (fan oven 180°C) for 5 minutes, or briefly in the microwave.

Navy beans *See* **Beans, dried**

Nectarines

Select unblemished fruit that give very slightly when gently squeezed. Avoid any that are hard or very soft.

To prepare

Skin, if liked, or wash. Halve, remove the stones (pits). Brush with lemon juice or slice and toss in lemon juice.

To freeze

Syrup-freezing: Make a light syrup using 225 g/8 oz/1 cup granulated sugar for every 600 ml/1 pt/2½ cups water. Add 1.5 ml/¼ tsp ascorbic acid or 15 ml/1 tbsp lemon juice. Pack the fruit in convenient quantities in rigid containers. Pour over just enough syrup to cover, leaving 2.5 cm/1 in headspace. Remove the air, seal, label and freeze.

STORAGE TIME: 12 months

To thaw and serve

Thaw in the fridge overnight, then use as required.

Non-stick baking parchment

This is ideal for layering foods that would otherwise stick together. It can also be used to wrap foods but they must then be overwrapped in foil or polythene bags to protect against moisture.

Nut cutlets

To prepare

Make in your usual way or buy commercially prepared ones.

To freeze

Wrap individually in clingfilm (plastic wrap), then in a polythene bag. Remove the air, seal, label and freeze. If commercially prepared in a vacuum pack, freeze as they are.

STORAGE TIME: 3 months

To thaw and serve

Thaw overnight in the fridge or at room temperature for 2–3 hours, then cook as usual. They can be cooked from frozen allowing an extra 5 minutes' cooking time.

Nut roasts

To prepare

Make in your usual way in a foil-lined dish. Cool quickly.

To freeze

Open-freeze until firm. Remove the dish, wrap in foil, seal, label and freeze.

STORAGE TIME: 3 months

To thaw and serve

Remove the wrappings and return to the dish. Thaw overnight in the fridge or at room temperature for 3–4 hours. Reheat in a moderate oven at 180°C/350°F/gas mark 4 (fan oven 160°C) for 30–45 minutes or until piping hot, or heat in the microwave on Full Power for 6–10 minutes.

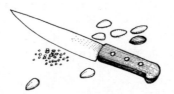

Nuts

Nuts such as brazils, walnuts, hazelnuts (filberts) and almonds can be stored in a cool dark cupboard in a sealed container for several months but they can be frozen if necessary.

To freeze

If in sealed bags, freeze as they are. Alternatively, tip into a polythene bag, remove the air, seal, label and freeze.

STORAGE TIME: 6 months

To thaw and serve

Use from frozen.

O

Ogen melon *See* **Melon**

Okra (ladies' fingers)

Select small pods, no more than 7.5 cm/3 in long.

To prepare

Trim off the stalks, but do not cut into the pods or they will ooze. Blanch in boiling water for 2 minutes. Drain and plunge immediately in a bowl of iced water to cool. Drain again and dry on kitchen paper (paper towels).

To freeze

Pack in convenient quantities in polythene bags. Remove the air, seal, label and freeze.

STORAGE TIME: 12 months

To thaw and serve

Use from frozen in soups, gumbos and curries, or cook from frozen in boiling, lightly salted water for about 6 minutes until just tender.

Olives

Olives keep well in the fridge but can be frozen. This is particularly useful if you've used half a can and want to keep the remainder and don't know when you want to use them. Olives with no liquid can be stored in a screw-topped jar, topped up with olive oil, in the fridge for several weeks.

To freeze

Empty the olives and their juice into rigid containers in convenient quantities, leaving 2.5 cm/1 in headspace. Remove the air, seal, label and freeze.

STORAGE TIME: 6 months

To thaw and serve

Thaw at room temperature for 2 hours, then use as required.

Onions

Prepared onions are a boon to any cook. It's also worth freezing shallots or pickling onions ready for later use.

Choose firm onions, whatever their size, with stiff, papery skins. Any that appear damp or are rotting or sprouting are not worth freezing.

To prepare
Peel, leave baby (pearl) onions whole, and slice or chop larger ones. Blanch in boiling water – 1 minute for chopped onions, 2 for sliced, 3 for whole ones. Drain and plunge immediately in a bowl of iced water to cool. Drain again and dry on kitchen paper (paper towels).

To freeze
Pack in convenient quantities in polythene bags or rigid containers. Remove the air, seal, label and freeze.
STORAGE TIME: 6 months

To thaw and use
Whole: Defrost at room temperature for about 2 hours before use.
Chopped or sliced: Thaw first or use from frozen as required.

Open-freezing
Open-freezing prevents the top of the food – such as a sauce topping on cooked dishes like lasagne or an iced (frosted) cake – being damaged by wrappers. It may also be used when you want frozen food to be free-flowing.
Made-up dishes: Simply freeze, unwrapped, in the container in which they were cooked. The dish may be lined with foil first so that it can be removed once frozen. When firm, remove the cooking dish, if liked, wrap the food securely in foil or a polythene bag, remove the air, seal, label and return to the freezer.
Free-flow foods: This is suitable for small fruits, vegetables, grated cheese, etc. Spread the food out in a single layer on a baking (cookie) sheet. Place in the freezer until firm. Tip into rigid containers or polythene bags. Remove the air, seal, label and return to the freezer.

Oranges

Orange rind, juice and flesh are all worth freezing, especially when you can buy cheap fruit. Select fruit that feel heavy for their size. Over-sized, light ones will be all pith and very little flesh or juice.

To prepare

Grate some of the rind. Thinly pare some for flavouring and garnishing. Cut off all the rind and pith, then cut the fruit into slices or segments.

To freeze

Rind: Pack in convenient quantities in small polythene bags or rigid containers. Remove the air, seal, label and freeze.

STORAGE TIME: 12 months

Fruit, dry-freezing, unsweetened: Spread out on a baking (cookie) sheet. Freeze until firm, then pack in polythene bags, seal, label and freeze.

STORAGE TIME: 12 months

Fruit, dry-freezing, sweetened: Layer the fruit in convenient quantities in rigid containers, sprinkling each layer with sugar to taste. Remove the air, seal, label and freeze.

STORAGE TIME: 12 months

Fruit, syrup-freezing: Make a light syrup using 225 g/8 oz/1 cup granulated sugar to every 600 ml/1 pt/2½ cups water. Pack the fruit in convenient quantities in rigid containers and just cover with syrup. Leave 2.5 cm/1 in headspace. Remove the air, seal, label and freeze.

STORAGE TIME: 12 months

Fruit, caramel-freezing: Make a caramel by heating 225 g/8 oz/1 cup granulated sugar in a saucepan, stirring gently until golden and melted. Immediately add 600 ml/1 pt/2½ cups water (take care, it will splutter), and stir over a gentle heat until dissolved. Leave to cool, then pack the fruit in convenient quantities in rigid containers. Pour over the caramel syrup, leaving 2.5 cm/1 in headspace. Remove the air, seal, label and freeze.

STORAGE TIME: 12 months

To thaw and serve

Rind: Use from frozen.
Fruit: Thaw overnight in the fridge or at room temperature for 2–3 hours.

See also **Seville oranges**

Oregano *See* **Herbs**

Ovenproof freezer ware

Dishes that are suitable for freezing and cooking food are very useful. Choose ceramic, pottery, heatproof glass or metal. If they are microwave-safe as well, then you have a three-way use! It is also useful to line the dish with foil for freezing the food, so that the dish can be removed for other use. The food can then be unwrapped and returned to the dish for cooking or reheating on removal from the freezer.

Oysters

Oysters can be frozen but only if they are very fresh. If in doubt, don't!

To prepare

Shuck, removing the top shell, being careful to retain the juice with the oyster in its half shell. If you are going to freeze the oysters cooked, tip them and their juices into a frying pan (skillet) and heat, stirring, until bubbling. Cool quickly. Scrub the shells and store.

To freeze

Raw: Arrange in a single layer on a baking (cookie) sheet and freeze until firm, taking care not to spill the juices. Pack in polythene bags or a rigid container, remove the air, seal, label and freeze.

STORAGE TIME: 1 month

Cooked: Pack the oysters in convenient quantities in polythene bags. Remove the air, seal, label and freeze.

STORAGE TIME: 1 month

To thaw and serve

Raw: Thaw in the fridge and eat as soon as thawed with a squeeze of lemon and a splash of Tabasco sauce, if liked. Alternatively, add a spoonful of cream, a good grinding of black pepper and a little grated Parmesan cheese to each and grill (broil) for 2–3 minutes until sizzling. Eat straight away.

Cooked: Add when still frozen to rice or pasta dishes or steak pie. Alternatively, thaw in the fridge overnight, then roll each in half a rasher (slice) of streaky bacon and grill (broil) until golden or use to stuff rump or fillet steaks before grilling.

P

Pak choi/soi

This oriental vegetable looks similar to baby Swiss chard.

To prepare

Trim the roots and quarter the heads lengthways. Wash under cold water and pat dry on kitchen paper (paper towels). Blanch in boiling water for 2 minutes. Drain and plunge immediately in a bowl of iced water to cool. Drain and pat dry on kitchen paper.

To freeze

Pack in convenient quantities in polythene bags or rigid containers. Remove the air, seal, label and freeze.

STORAGE TIME: 12 months

To thaw and serve

Cook from frozen in boiling, lightly salted water for 3 minutes, then drain well. Alternatively, stir-fry from frozen.

Pancakes

Pancakes freeze beautifully either plain or stuffed (but avoid stuffings that contain foods that don't freeze, such as hard-boiled eggs or mayonnaise).

To prepare

Make in your usual way, layering each one with a piece of non-stick baking parchment. Cool.

To freeze

Plain: Pack in convenient quantities in a polythene bag. Remove the air, seal, label and freeze.

STORAGE TIME: 6 months

Stuffed: Fill with your chosen filling. Place in a single layer in a foil container or a dish lined with foil. Cover with foil, label and freeze until firm. Alternatively, freeze in a dish, then remove it once frozen and wrap the pancakes tightly in labelled foil, then return to the freezer.

STORAGE TIME: 3 months

To thaw and serve

Plain: Wrap stacks of 4 frozen pancakes in foil and reheat in a hot oven at 200°C/400°F/gas mark 6 (fan oven 180°C) for about 15 minutes. Alternatively, thaw at room temperature for 2–3 hours, then use as required, or wrap in non-stick baking parchment or kitchen paper (paper towels) and reheat in the microwave on Full Power for 3–4 minutes, if frozen or 1–2 minutes if thawed, turning the stack once. Use as required.

Stuffed: If frozen in a dish, unwrap, return to the dish and cover with foil again. Otherwise, leave in their foil wrapper. Cook in a moderately hot oven at 190°C/375°F/gas mark 5 (fan oven 170°C) for about 35–40 minutes until piping hot through. Serve with a sauce, if liked.

Papaya

Select fresh-smelling, firm, undamaged fruit.

To prepare

Peel, halve, remove the black seeds and cut the fruit into slices or dice.

To freeze

Dry-freezing, sweetened: Pack the fruit in convenient quantities in rigid containers, layering with 100 g/4 oz/½ cup caster (superfine) sugar for every 2–3 fruit. Remove the air, seal, label and freeze.

STORAGE TIME: 6 months

Syrup-freezing: Make a light syrup using 225 g/8 oz/1 cup granulated sugar to every 600 ml/1 pt/2½ cups water. Pack the fruit in convenient quantities in rigid containers. Add just enough syrup to cover, leaving 2.5 cm/1 in headspace. Remove the air, seal, label and freeze.

STORAGE TIME: 6 months

Purée-freezing: Purée the fruit in a blender or food processor and sweeten to taste. Pack in rigid containers in convenient quantities, leaving 2.5 cm/1 in headspace. Remove the air, seal, label and freeze.

STORAGE TIME: 6 months

To thaw and serve

Thaw in the fridge overnight or at room temperature for 2–3 hours. Use as required.

Paper towels   *See* **Kitchen paper**

Parma ham *See* **Ham, raw, cured**

Parmesan cheese *See* **Cheese, hard**

Parsley *See* **Herbs**

Parsnips

Home-grown parsnips are best left in the ground. It's only worth freezing commercially grown ones if you find bargains.

To prepare

Scrape or peel, then cut into slices or wedges. Blanch in boiling water for 2 minutes. Drain and plunge immediately in a bowl of iced water to cool. Drain again and dry on kitchen paper (paper towels).

To freeze

Pack in convenient quantities in polythene bags. Remove the air, seal, label and freeze.

STORAGE TIME: 12 months

To thaw and serve

Cook from frozen in boiling, lightly salted water for about 8 minutes until tender. Alternatively, thaw at room temperature for 2–3 hours or blanch in boiling water for 2–3 minutes, then roast in the oven in your usual way.

Partridge

There are two types, the English, or grey, partridge and the French red leg.

To prepare

If not already prepared, hang for 3 days, pluck and draw and remove the head and feet. Keep the neck, gizzard, heart and liver and put in a small polythene bag. Wash the bird inside and out with cold water and pat dry with kitchen paper (paper towels). Truss.

To freeze

Protect the bone ends with foil, then pack in a polythene bag with the bag of giblets. Remove the air, seal, label and freeze.

STORAGE TIME: Birds 6 months, giblets 3 months

To thaw and serve

Thaw in the fridge for up to 24 hours and cook as soon as defrosted.

Passion fruit

These small, round fruit should be purple and wrinkly and should feel heavy for their size.

To prepare

Cut into halves and scoop out the juicy pulp and the seeds. Weigh the seeds and pulp and mix with half their weight of caster (superfine) sugar (e.g. if you have 100 g/4 oz/½ cup pulp and seeds, add 50 g/2 oz/¼ cup sugar).

To freeze

Spoon in convenient quantities into small, rigid containers. Remove the air, seal, label and freeze.

STORAGE TIME: 12 months

To thaw and serve

Thaw in the fridge overnight or at room temperature for about 1 hour, then add to fruit salads, serve with whipped cream or spoon over ice cream.

Pasta

Cooked pasta can be frozen either plain or in made-up dishes. It is useful for a quick supper, either reheated or cold as a salad.

To prepare

Cook in your usual way, reducing the cooking time by 1–2 minutes. If cooked completely, it will be too soft when thawed. Drain, rinse with cold water and drain again. Dry on kitchen paper (paper towels).

To freeze

Pack in convenient quantities in polythene bags. Remove the air, seal, label and freeze.

STORAGE TIME: 2 months

To thaw and serve

Plunge, still frozen, into boiling, lightly salted water for 1–2 minutes. Drain and serve.

See also **Cannelloni, Lasagne, Macaroni cheese**

Pastry (paste) *See individual entries, e.g.* **Choux pastry,** *etc.*

Also **Batch baking, Flan cases, Pies, Vol au vents,** *etc.*

Pâtés

All pâtés freeze well but should be eaten as soon as possible once thawed. If making your own, avoid using too much garlic. Flavours can alter after freezing, and garlic, in particular, can taste musty if too much is used.

To prepare

Make in your usual way and cook in a terrine or loaf tin (pan), lined with foil. Cool quickly. Leave whole, or cut into slices. Alternatively, make the pâté in individual portions in ramekin dishes (custard cups).

To freeze

Whole: Wrap in foil and freeze until firm. Remove the container. Wrap in foil and overwrap in a polythene bag. Remove the air, seal, label and return to the freezer.

STORAGE TIME: 2 months, 1 month if covered in bacon

Slices: Wrap each slice individually in clingfilm (plastic wrap) or foil. Overwrap in a polythene bag. Remove the air, seal, label and freeze.

STORAGE TIME: 2 months

Individual: Wrap completely in foil, label and freeze.

STORAGE TIME: 2 months

To thaw and serve

Whole: Thaw whole pâtés in the fridge overnight.

Slices: Thaw at room temperature for 1–2 hours.

Individual: Thaw overnight in the fridge or at room temperature for about 2–3 hours.

Pavlovas

Pavlovas will keeep for up to 2 weeks in a sealed container in a cool place, but can also be frozen.

To prepare

Make in your usual way and leave to cool.

To freeze

Carefully transfer to a rigid container. I do this by placing the pavlova on the inside of the lid, then invert the container over the top to cover. Label carefully so you don't forget this! Seal and freeze. Take care when storing as it will still be very fragile.

STORAGE TIME: 12 months

To thaw and serve

Fill while still frozen and thaw at room temperature. Serve within 2–3 hours.

Pawpaw *See* **Papaya**

Peaches

Select unblemished fruit that give very slightly when gently squeezed. Avoid any that are hard or very soft.

To prepare

Skin, if liked, or wash. Halve, remove the stones (pits). Brush with lemon juice or slice and toss in lemon juice.

To freeze

Syrup-freezing: Make a light syrup using 225 g/8 oz/1 cup granulated sugar to every 600 ml/1 pt/2½ cups water. Add 1.5 ml/¼ tsp ascorbic acid or 15 ml/1 tbsp lemon juice. Pack the fruit in convenient quantities in rigid containers. Pour over just enough syrup to cover, leaving 2.5 cm/1 in headspace. Remove the air, seal, label and freeze.

STORAGE TIME: 12 months

To thaw and serve

Thaw in the fridge overnight, then use as required.

Pears

Choose pears that are just ripe or slightly under-ripe. Avoid any that are bruised.

To prepare

They are only worth freezing if poached first. Peel, then leave whole or quarter and core. Make a syrup using 175 g/6 oz/¾ cup granulated sugar to every 600 ml/1 pt/2½ cups water (or half water and half red or white wine or cider). Poach the fruit gently in the syrup for about 5–10 minutes for quarters, 15–30 minutes for whole ones, depending on ripeness, turning whole ones halfway through poaching. Cool quickly.

To freeze

Put in convenient quantities in rigid containers, leaving 2.5 cm/1 in headspace. Make sure the fruit is covered by the syrup. Remove the air, seal, label and freeze.

STORAGE TIME: 12 months

To thaw and serve

Thaw in the fridge overnight or thaw at room temperature for 3–4 hours. If serving hot, transfer to a saucepan and heat gently until melted, then bring to the boil and simmer until hot through.

Peas

Commercially frozen peas are so good that it's only worth freezing fresh ones if you have a glut in your garden. Select tender young peas in smooth, shiny pods.

To prepare

Shell the peas. Blanch in boiling water for 1 minute. Drain, then plunge immediately in a bowl of iced water to cool. Drain again and dry on kitchen paper (paper towels).

To freeze

Pack in convenient quantities in polythene bags. Remove the air, seal, label and freeze.

STORAGE TIME: 12 months

To thaw and serve

Cook from frozen in boiling, lightly salted water for about 5 minutes until just tender.

Pease pudding

To prepare
Make in your usual way. Cool quickly.

To freeze
Spoon in convenient quantities into rigid containers. Remove the air, seal, label and freeze.

STORAGE TIME: 12 months

To thaw and serve
Thaw overnight in the fridge or at room temperature for 3–4 hours, then reheat in a saucepan. Alternatively, reheat from frozen on Full Power in the microwave, breaking up the block as soon as possible and stirring frequently until piping hot.

Peppers (bell peppers)
Peppers freeze well unblanched but for longer-term storage it is better to take the time to blanch them first. Select firm, shiny peppers of any colour.

To prepare, unblanched
Wash and pat dry on kitchen paper (paper towels). Leave as they are or cut off the stalks and remove the seeds.

To freeze
Wrap in polythene bags. Remove the air, seal, label and freeze.

STORAGE TIME: 2 months

To prepare, blanched
Cut off the tops and remove the seeds. Leave whole, slice or dice. Blanch whole peppers in boiling water for 3 minutes, slices or dice for 1 minute. Drain and plunge immediately in a bowl of iced water to cool. Drain again and dry on kitchen paper. Stuff now, if liked.

To freeze
Whole, plain, and sliced or diced: Pack in convenient quantities in polythene bags. Remove the air, seal, label and freeze.

STORAGE TIME: 12 months

Whole, stuffed: Pack in convenient quantities in polythene bags. Remove the air, seal, label and freeze.

STORAGE TIME: 3 months

To thaw and serve

Whole, unblanched: If unseeded, cut off the tops, remove the seeds, cut up as necessary and cooked from frozen. If already seeded, cut up if necessary and cook from frozen. Alternatively, stuff and cook from frozen in your usual way, allowing an extra 4–5 minutes' cooking time to allow for thawing.

Whole, blanched: If not already stuffed, fill with stuffing now and cook from frozen, allowing an extra 4–5 minutes' cooking time for thawing.

Whole, blanched, stuffed: Allow to thaw for 2–3 hours at room temperature, then cook in your usual way.

Sliced or diced, blanched: Use from frozen.

Persimmons

Persimmons are becoming more widely available. They are ideal for adding extra flavour to plainer fruits like pears or apples and are delicious served with ice cream. Select ripe orange fruit with unblemished skins.

To prepare

Peel off the skins and leave whole or cut into slices.

To freeze

Dry-freezing, whole: Wrap individual fruit in clingfilm (plastic wrap), then foil. Label and freeze.

STORAGE TIME: 2 months

Syrup-freezing, slices: Make a heavy sugar syrup using 350 g/12 oz/ 1½ cups granulated sugar for every 600 ml/1 pt/2½ cups water. Pack the slices in rigid containers in convenient quantities. Pour over just enough syrup to cover, leaving 2.5 cm/1 in headspace. Remove the air, seal, label and freeze.

STORAGE TIME: 12 months

To thaw and serve

Whole and slices: Thaw in the fridge overnight or at room temperature for about 3 hours. Use as required.

Pet food

Pet food can be frozen but it is vital that you keep it separate from human food. Pet meat production doesn't have the rigorous hygiene standards that our food is subjected to and cross-contamination could occur. It can be frozen raw or cooked – I prefer to cook it first.

To prepare and freeze
Cook if liked. Divide into convenient quantities and pack in polythene bags. Remove the air, seal, label and freeze. Pack the bags in a large, clean polythene bag for extra protection.
STORAGE TIME: 3 months

To thaw and use
Raw: Thaw at room temperature, then cook. Alternatively, cook from frozen. Make sure it is thoroughly cooked through. Cool quickly and store in a sealed container in the fridge for up to 3 days.
Cooked: Thaw in the fridge overnight. Keep in a sealed container away from food for humans. Use within 3 days.

Pheasant

Pheasant are usually sold in pairs – a cock and a hen. The hen is usually smaller and more tender. A large cock bird will serve up to 4 people, a hen 2–3 people. The season is from October to January.

To prepare
If not ready-prepared, hang for 3–10 days, then pluck and draw and remove the head and feet. Keep the neck, gizzard, heart and liver and put in a small polythene bag. Wash the bird inside and out with cold water and pat dry with kitchen paper (paper towels). Truss.

To freeze
Protect the bone ends with foil, then pack in a polythene bag with the bag of giblets. Remove the air, seal, label and freeze. Pack in convenient quantities in polythene bags. Remove the air, seal, label and freeze.
STORAGE TIME: Birds 6 months, giblets 3 months

To thaw and serve
Thaw in the fridge for up to 24 hours and cook as soon as defrosted.

Pies

Both sweet and savoury pies freeze beautifully either raw, to be cooked fresh when thawed, or cooked, ready to reheat or eat cold.

To prepare
Make in your usual way. Ideally, use foil dishes or plates for large ones and tartlet tins (patty pans) and individual foil cases for small ones. If you make a large pie in an ordinary pie dish, you may have to leave it in the dish until you cook it – they can't be removed as easily as other cooked dishes. Make sure any filling is cold before you put it into the pies.

To freeze
Open-freeze until firm. Remove individual pies from tartlet tins and pack in polythene bags. Wrap large ones in foil or polythene bags. Remove the air, seal, label and return to the freezer.
STORAGE TIME: Meat or fish pies 3 months, fruit and sweet pies 6 months

To thaw and serve
Remove the wrappers, glaze the top with milk or egg, if liked, and cook from frozen according to the recipe. Add on extra cooking time to allow for defrosting (up to 30 minutes, depending on the filling). If the top is over-browning, cover it loosely with foil during cooking.

Pie shells   *See* **Flan cases** *and* **Shortcrust pastry**

Pigeon

Pigeons freeze well. They can be roasted but I prefer them casseroled or braised – it ensures their tenderness. Allow one per person.

To prepare
If not ready-prepared, pluck and draw. Wash in cold water, then dry inside and out with kitchen paper (paper towels). If keeping the giblets, reserve the heart, liver, neck and gizzard and pack in a separate polythene bag.

To freeze
Protect the bone ends with foil, then pack in polythene bags. Add the bag of giblets. Remove the air, seal, label and freeze.
STORAGE TIME: Birds 6 months, giblets 3 months

To thaw and serve
Thaw in the fridge for up to 24 hours and cook as soon as defrosted.

Pineapple

Fresh pineapple freezes well. Select ripe fruit that gives slightly when pressed, with a sweet, fresh smell. Avoid any that feel very soft or are completely hard. You can also freeze leftover canned pineapple. Large cans of pineapple are cheaper than small ones, so I always buy a large one, use what I need, then freeze the remainder.

To prepare

Fresh pineapple: Cut off the green top and base, then, holding the fruit upright, cut off all the skin from top to bottom with a sharp knife. Cut into slices and remove the core if hard. Trim off any 'eyes' that remain.

Canned: No preparation necessary.

To freeze

Fresh, dry-freezing, unsweetened: Lay the slices on a baking (cookie) sheet. Open-freeze until firm. Pack in polythene bags. Remove the air, seal, label and return to the freezer.

STORAGE TIME: 3 months

Fresh, dry-freezing, sweetened: Layer the fruit in convenient quantities in rigid containers, sprinkling each layer with caster (superfine) sugar. Allow about 175 g/6 oz/¾ cup sugar per medium pineapple. Remove the air, seal, label and freeze.

STORAGE TIME: 12 months

Fresh, syrup-freezing: Make a heavy syrup, using 350 g/12 oz/1½ cups granulated sugar for every 600 ml/1 pt/2½ cups water. Pack the fruit in convenient quantities in rigid containers. Pour over just enough syrup to cover. Leave 2.5 cm/1 in headspace. Remove the air, seal, label and freeze.

STORAGE TIME: 12 months

Canned: Put in convenient quantities in a rigid container with any juice. Leave 2.5 cm/1 in headspace. Remove the air, seal, label and freeze.

STORAGE TIME: 12 months

To thaw and serve

Thaw overnight in the fridge and use as required.

Pitta breads

To prepare and freeze
Overwrap in a polythene bag. Remove the air, seal, label and freeze.
STORAGE TIME: 6 months

To thaw and serve
Heat from frozen in the toaster, under the grill (broiler) or in the microwave just to soften. Do not allow to crisp. Split, then open and fill with desired filling, or cut into fingers to serve as a bread accompaniment. Alternatively, if serving cold, thaw at room temperature individually for about 1 hour.

Pizzas
Pizzas are best frozen unbaked, but leftover cooked slices can be frozen. Bought pizzas should be frozen according to manufacturer's instructions.

To prepare
Make in your usual way, place on a baking (cookie) sheet, but do not bake.

To freeze
Open-freeze until firm. Wrap in clingfilm (plastic wrap) and overwrap tightly in foil. Label, then return to the freezer.
STORAGE TIME: Meat-topped 2 months, vegetable-topped 3 months

To thaw and serve
Return to the baking sheet. Bake from frozen in a hot oven at 220°C/425°F/gas mark 7 (fan oven 190°C) until golden and bubbling. Alternatively, thaw at room temperature for 2–3 hours, then cook.

Plaice
Check with your fishmonger that the fish has not been previously frozen. The flesh should be firm with a fresh smell. If whole, the eyes should be bright.

To prepare
Rinse with cold water and pat dry on kitchen paper (paper towels). Whole fish may be filleted.

To freeze
Interleave with polythene interleave sheets or clingfilm (plastic wrap), then pack in polythene bags, remove the air, seal, label and freeze.
STORAGE TIME: 3 months

To thaw and serve

Trim the fins and tails of whole fish. Thaw at room temperature for 2 hours before cooking in your usual way, or cook from frozen, allowing 3–5 minutes' extra cooking time.

Plated meals

Plated meals – especially the Sunday roast – are ideal for individual midweek meals. I always cook extra vegetables to make sure I've got enough over! Plain boiled old potatoes don't freeze well (although new ones do), so roast or mash them or make duchesse potatoes.

To prepare

Plate up a complete meal, keeping the less dense foods towards the centre of the plate (in case you want to reheat in the microwave), and spoon gravy over the meat.

To freeze

Cover tightly with clingfilm (plastic wrap), then in foil. Label and freeze.
STORAGE TIME: 3 months

To thaw and serve

Ideally, thaw in the fridge overnight, or at room temperature for 2–3 hours, then unwrap. Put the plate over a pan of boiling water. Cover with the saucepan lid or foil and steam for 10 minutes or until piping hot. Alternatively, remove the clingfilm, then re-wrap tightly in foil and reheat in a moderately hot oven at 190°C/375°F/gas mark 5 (fan oven 170°C) for about 20 minutes until hot through. They may also be reheated in the microwave. Remove the foil, roll the clingfilm back slightly at one edge and microwave on Full Power for about 4 minutes (depending on the quantity and power output) until hot through. To test, feel the bottom of the plate in the centre: it should feel boiling hot. If not, heat a little longer.

Plums

The skins of plums may toughen on thawing. If this is unpalatable, purée the fruit before freezing. Select ripe, unblemished fruit.

To prepare

Wash, halve and remove the stones (pits) or leave whole, if preferred.

To freeze

Dry-freezing, sweetened: Pack in layers in convenient quantities, sprinkling caster (superfine) sugar between each layer. Use about 225 g/ 8 oz/1 cup sugar per 450 g/1 lb fruit. Remove the air, seal, label and freeze.

STORAGE TIME: 12 months

Syrup-freezing: Make a heavy syrup using 350 g/12 oz/1½ cups granulated sugar to every 600 ml/1 pt/2½ cups water. Pack the plums in convenient quantities in rigid containers, leaving 2.5 cm/1 in headspace. Pour just enough syrup over to cover the fruit. Remove the air, seal, label and freeze.

STORAGE TIME: 12 months

Purée-freezing: Put just enough water in a saucepan to cover the base. Add the stoned (pitted) fruit, cover and cook gently until the fruit is tender, stirring occasionally. Purée in a blender or food processor or pass through a fine sieve (strainer) and sweeten to taste. Pour in convenient quantities in rigid containers, leaving 2.5 cm/1 in headspace. Remove the air, seal, label and freeze.

STORAGE TIME: 12 months

To thaw and serve

Thaw at room temperature for about 3 hours, then use as required.

Polenta (cornmeal)

Polenta tends to go a bit sticky and granular on thawing, so I don't really recommend freezing it – instead I buy precooked cornmeal that can be cooked in 5 minutes. But if you have some left over, you can freeze it for short periods, then serve it with lots of Parmesan cheese or coated in tomato sauce.

To prepare
Make in your usual way. Leave to cool and cut into slices.

To freeze
Wrap individually in clingfilm (plastic wrap), then place in a polythene bag. Remove the air, seal, label and freeze.
STORAGE TIME: 2 months

To thaw and serve
Thaw at room temperature for 1–2 hours, then cover with cheese or tomato sauce and reheat in a moderate oven at 180°C/350°F/gas mark 4 (fan oven 160°C) for 15–25 minutes or until piping hot. Alternatively, fry (sauté) the slices in a little olive oil or grill (broil) the slices, brushed with oil, until golden on both sides and hot through.

Pomegranates

Pomegranates are only available during the winter months. Freeze them then for use at other times. Remember that it's the juice that has the delicious flavour – the seeds and pith are bitter. Select well-rounded fruit with firm skins and the minimum of blemishes.

To prepare
Cut into halves, scoop out all the seeds and juice into a sieve (strainer) over a bowl. Rub the juice through and pour into ice cube trays. Freeze until firm, tip into a polythene bag, remove the air, seal, label and return to the freezer.
STORAGE TIME: 12 months

To thaw and serve
Thaw in the fridge overnight or at room temperature for 1–2 hours. Use the juice to flavour fruit salads, as a sauce over ice cream or added to orange or apple juice as a nutritious drink.

Poppadoms

Uncooked poppadoms have a long use-by date and they take seconds to cook, so there is no point in freezing them.

Pork

Buy a side of pork or half a pig for freezing if you can. Otherwise buy joints and cuts when on offer. Do remember that if you buy a half animal, it will include belly, hand and spring (the front leg and shoulder, often cut as one large joint), trotters and half a head! If you aren't going to use these, it would be better to negotiate with your butcher the cuts you require. Discuss what you want and how you want it or you'll end up wasting money rather than saving it. Ask your butcher to pack and label meat in the quantities you require.

To prepare and freeze

Wrapped joints and sealed packs of pork meat: Meat bought like this from the supermarket need only overwrapping in polythene bags, then sealing, labelling and freezing.

Unwrapped meat: Interleave chops, escalopes, etc. with polythene interleave sheets or non-stick baking parchment, or wrap them individually in clingfilm (plastic wrap). Wrap in convenient quantities in polythene bags, then remove the air, seal, label and freeze.

STORAGE TIME: Joints, chops, steaks and escalopes 9 months, diced stewing or casserole meat and rashers 4 months, minced (ground) pork 3 months

To thaw and serve

Joints: Thaw joints overnight in the fridge or at room temperature for 2–6 hours according to size, then cook as required. Do not cook from frozen.

Steaks, chops and escalopes: Cook from frozen or thaw first for 2–4 hours at room temperature or overnight in the fridge.

Minced pork: Can be cooked from frozen in a saucepan or the microwave, scraping off the browned meat as it cooks, breaking up the lump as soon as possible and making sure all the grains are separate and no longer pink, before adding any remaining ingredients.

See also **Casseroles** *and* **Meat, cooked**

Potatoes

It is not worth freezing old potatoes as they are convenient to store. However, you can freeze new potatoes to enjoy out of season, and prepared potatoes. Select small, even-sized new potatoes that are very fresh and firm.

To prepare

Scrub or scrape the new potatoes. Blanch in boiling water for 2 minutes. Drain and plunge immediately in a bowl of iced water to cool. Drain and dry on kitchen paper (paper towels). Alternatively, boil in lightly salted water with a sprig of mint added, until still slightly undercooked. Drain and toss in butter. Cool quickly.

To freeze

Pack in convenient quantities in polythene bags. Remove the air, seal, label and freeze.

STORAGE TIME: Raw 12 months, cooked 3 months

To thaw and serve

Blanched: Cook from frozen in boiling, lightly salted water, with a sprig of mint added, for up to 10 minutes until tender. Drain and toss in butter and chopped fresh parsley.

Cooked: Thaw at room temperature for 2–3 hours, then heat gently.

Potatoes, chips (fries)

To prepare

Peel and cut up the potatoes in your usual way. Heat oil for deep-frying to 190°C/375°F or until a cube of day-old bread browns in 30 seconds. Cook in large batches for 2 minutes until slightly softened but not browned. Drain well. Spread out on baking (cookie) sheets and leave to cool.

To freeze

Open-freeze until firm, then pack in convenient quantities in polythene bags. Alternatively, as they will be free-flow, you can store them in a large bag if you prefer. Remove the air, seal, label and return to the freezer.

STORAGE TIME: 4 months

To thaw and serve

Cook from frozen. Deep-fry in your usual way until crisp and golden brown. Drain on kitchen paper (paper towels) before serving.

Potatoes, croquette

To prepare
Make in your usual way. Roll in dried breadcrumbs.

To freeze
Place on a baking (cookie) sheet. Open-freeze until firm. Pack in rigid containers. Remove the air, seal, label and freeze.
STORAGE TIME: 3 months

To thaw and serve
Thaw at room temperature for 2–3 hours. Deep-fry for about 4 minutes until golden, then drain on kitchen paper (paper towels).

Potatoes, duchesse

To prepare
Prepare in your usual way and pipe on to non-stick baking parchment on a baking (cookie) sheet. Open-freeze until firm. Pack in rigid containers. Remove the air, seal, label and freeze.
STORAGE TIME: 3 months

To thaw and serve
Place on a lightly greased baking (cookie) sheet. Brush with beaten egg to glaze, if liked. Bake in a hot oven at 220°C/425°F/gas mark 7 (fan oven 200°C) for about 15–20 minutes, until golden and hot through.

Potatoes, stuffed jacket-baked
These can be frozen but there is little time saved unless you cook them first in the microwave.

To prepare
Scrub, prick and cook the potatoes in your usual way, then stuff according to the recipe. Leave to cool.

To freeze
Pack in rigid containers. Remove the air, seal, label and freeze.
STORAGE TIME: 3 months

To thaw and serve

Thaw at room temperature for 2–3 hours, then cook straight away in a hot oven at 200°C/400°F/gas mark 6 (fan oven 180°C) for about 20 minutes or until golden on top and piping hot.

Alternatively, thaw and reheat in the microwave on Medium until hot through, rearranging the potatoes once during heating, then flash under a hot grill (broiler) to brown the tops.

Poussins (Cornish hens) *See* **Chicken**

Prawns (shrimp)

There are many varieties of prawns available ready-frozen. But sometimes bargains are to be had on the fresh fish counter – such as langoustines or raw tiger prawns (jumbo shrimp). Check with your fishmonger that they are very fresh and they have not been previously frozen. They must be frozen as soon as you get them home.

All prawns should be firm and plump. Raw ones will be bluish-grey, cooked ones a bright pink colour. They should smell sweet and pleasantly fishy.

To prepare

Rinse under cold water and pat dry on kitchen paper (paper towels).

To freeze

Pack in convenient quantities in polythene bags. Remove the air, seal, label and freeze.

STORAGE TIME: 1 month

To thaw and serve

Cooked: Thaw cooked prawns in the fridge overnight or at room temperature for 1–2 hours, then use immediately. They can be added from frozen to cooked dishes, but remember they will add a quantity of liquid to the finished dish as they thaw.

Raw: Cook from frozen in your usual way just until they turn pink.

Profiteroles *See* **Eclairs and profiteroles**

Puff pastry (paste)

Keep ready-made frozen puff pastry in the freezer for use as required – it's not worth making your own!

To thaw and use
Thaw at room temperature for 1–2 hours, then use as required.

Pulses *See* **Beans, dried, Peas, dried,** *and* **Lentils**

Pumpkins

Pumpkins are a particularly good buy just after Hallowe'en.

To prepare
Halve, scoop out the seeds, peel and dice or slice. Cook in your usual way until tender. Drain, rinse with cold water, then drain again and cool quickly. Leave in cubes or mash, as required.

To freeze
Pack in convenient quantities in rigid containers. Remove the air, seal, label and freeze.

STORAGE TIME: 12 months

To thaw and serve
Cubes: Steam from frozen over a pan of hot water until hot through.
Mashed: Thaw at room temperature, then use in pies, soups, etc.

Purée-freezing

Many fruit and vegetables can be puréed for freezing. This takes up less space and is ideal for those that would need puréeing before use in made-up dishes or sauces.

To prepare

Cook, if necessary. Juicy fruits can be puréed raw. Purée in a blender or food processor, then pass through a sieve (strainer), if necessary, to remove any seeds or strings. Sweeten the purée with sugar, if appropriate. Other flavourings (e.g. cinnamon in fruits) should be added when the purée has defrosted.

To freeze

Pack in convenient quantities in rigid containers, leaving 2.5 cm/1 in headspace. Remove the air, seal, label and freeze.

STORAGE TIME: 12 months

To thaw and serve

Thaw at room temperature for 1–2 hours, or heat from frozen in a saucepan or in the microwave.

See also individual fruits, e.g. **Raspberries**

Puy lentils *See* **Lentils**

q

Quail

Quail are now farmed in the UK and available all year round. Freeze when bargains are available. Choose plump birds, allowing one per person.

To prepare

They are usually sold undrawn but clean them, if you prefer, before freezing and put the heart, gizzard and liver in a small polythene bag to freeze separately from the bird. Rinse inside and out with cold water and pat dry on kitchen paper (paper towels). Truss.

To freeze

Protect the bone ends with foil, then pack in a polythene bag with the bag of giblets.Remove the air, seal, label and freeze.

STORAGE TIME: Cleaned birds 6 months, giblets and undrawn birds 3 months

To thaw and serve

Thaw in the fridge for up to 24 hours and cook as soon as defrosted.

Quails' eggs

These little eggs are often hard-boiled (hard-cooked) for use as a starter or in salads. Do not freeze them in this state. They can, however, be frozen raw, without their shells, ready to be baked in little tartlets or other delicacies.

To prepare and freeze

Break into small foil or plastic containers. Freeze singly or in pairs. Remove the air, seal, label and freeze. You may also be able to freeze them broken individually in deep ice cube trays. Cover the tray with clingfilm (plastic wrap), then, once frozen, tip them into a rigid container, remove the air, seal, label and freeze.

STORAGE TIME: 6 months

To thaw and use

Thaw in the fridge for several hours or at room temperature for 1–2 hours. Use as fresh quail's eggs.

Quantities

Foods are best frozen in quantities that can be used in one go, so don't freeze entire packs of 16 chops, 24 chicken legs, etc. unless you intend to use them for a party.

There is a limit to the quantity of food that can be frozen at one time, usually up to 10 per cent of the total capacity, but this varies according to the size of the freezer, so check your manufacturer's instruction booklet. Do not try to exceed this quantity – the temperature of the freezer may rise above the safe limit, causing bacteria to flourish.

Quark

Quark does not freeze well; it becomes grainy on thawing.

Queen scallops

These little scallops are available ready-frozen so can be put straight in the freezer. Usually, those on the fresh fish counter have been previously frozen and thawed, so should not be home-frozen.

Quiches and gougères

Cooked quiches and gougères freeze very well. Always reheat before serving.

To prepare

Make and cook in your usual way, quiches in a flan ring or dish (preferably a foil one), set on a baking (cookie) sheet, gougères in an oven-to-freezer dish. Cool.

To freeze

Wrap the quiche or gougère and its container completely in foil or a polythene bag. Remove the air, seal, label and freeze. Quiches in flan rings should be open-frozen, then removed from the ring, wrapped and frozen as before.

STORAGE TIME: 6 months, 3 months if containing bacon

To thaw and serve

If made in a flan ring, put the flan back on a baking sheet and replace the ring. Reheat all quiches and gougères from frozen in a moderate oven at 180°C/350°F/gas mark 4 (fan oven 160°C) for about 30 minutes until piping hot. Serve hot or leave to cool before serving.

Quinces

Quinces are usually made into jelly (clear conserve) and cheeses but they can be frozen in lemon syrup. They also make a delicious addition to apple pies. Select even-sized bright yellow fruits with unblemished skins.

To prepare
Peel and core, then slice or dice. Mix with 15 ml/1 tbsp lemon juice to every 3–4 fruit to prevent browning.

To freeze
Dry-freezing, unsweetened: Spread out on a baking (cookie) sheet and freeze until firm. Pack in polythene bags. Remove the air, seal, label and return to the freezer.
STORAGE TIME: 12 months
Syrup-freezing: Make a heavy syrup using 350 g/12 oz/1½ cups granulated sugar to 600 ml/1 pt/2½ cups water. Pare the rind of a small lemon and add with 700 g/1½ lb quinces. Poach for 20 minutes until almost tender. Cool quickly, then pack in convenient quantities in rigid containers, leaving 2.5 cm/1 in headspace. Remove the air, seal, label and freeze.
STORAGE TIME: 12 months

To thaw and serve
Dry-frozen pieces: Thaw at room temperature for 2–3 hours.
Syrup-frozen: Reheat from frozen and simmer for about 5 minutes, then serve warm or cold.

Quorn

Quorn is sold ready-frozen and should be transferred to the freezer as soon as possible. It is also available in the chiller cabinet.

To freeze
Freeze in its packaging, but remember to label first.
STORAGE TIME: 3 months

To thaw and serve
Cook according to packet directions if bought frozen. If from the chiller cabinet, thaw at room temperature for 2–3 hours or overnight in the fridge, then cook as soon as possible.

r

Rabbit

To prepare
If not ready-prepared, clean the rabbit but leave on its fur, then hang it for 2–3 days, if liked. If young and fairly small, there is no need to hang. Skin and leave whole, or cut into halves or quarters as required. Rinse with cold water and pat dry on kitchen paper (paper towels).

To freeze
Raw: Wrap in foil to protect the bone ends, then place in a polythene bag, remove the air, seal, label and freeze.

STORAGE TIME: 6 months

Cooked: Casserole or stew the rabbit in your usual way. Cool quickly. Turn into a rigid container, remove the air, seal, label and freeze or line a casserole dish (Dutch oven) with foil, then add the cold, cooked food. Open-freeze until firm. Remove the dish. Overwrap the block of casseroled food in more foil or place in a polythene bag. Remove the air, seal, label and freeze.

STORAGE TIME: 3 months

To thaw and serve
Raw: Thaw in the fridge overnight or at room temperature for several hours, then cook in your usual way.

Cooked: Thaw at room temperature for 4–5 hours, then turn into a saucepan or a casserole dish (Dutch oven), removing all packaging, and reheat in a preheated oven at 180°C/350°F/gas mark 4 (fan oven 160°C) for about 45 minutes until piping hot. Alternatively, thaw in the microwave in the rigid container or remove the foil packaging and turn into a microwave-safe casserole dish. Microwave on Medium–low for 15–20 minutes, stirring frequently. Then cook on Full Power for about 15 minutes until piping hot, stirring occasionally.

Radish, summer
This is not suitable for freezing.

Radish, winter

Choose long, plump, firm roots with clean, black skin.

To prepare

Wash, peel and coarsely grate or dice. Blanch dice in boiling water for 2 minutes, grated for 1 minute. Drain and plunge immediately in a bowl of iced water to cool. Drain again and dry on kitchen paper (paper towels).

To freeze

Grated: Pack in convenient quantities in polythene bags. Remove the air, seal, label and freeze.

STORAGE TIME: 3 months

Dice: Pack in convenient quantities in polythene bags. Remove the air, seal, label and freeze.

STORAGE TIME: 6 months

To thaw and serve

Grated: Thaw at room temperature for 1–2 hours. Dry on kitchen paper and dress with mayonnaise or French dressing.

Diced: Cook from frozen in boiling, lightly salted water for 6–8 minutes until tender. Drain and toss with butter or mix with parsley sauce.

Raspberries

Select ripe fruit that haven't gone mushy. If over-ripe, they won't freeze well.

To prepare

Pick over and remove any stalks. Discard any damaged fruit.

To freeze

Dry-freezing, unsweetened: Spread out on a baking (cookie) sheet, open-freeze until firm, then pack in polythene bags. Alternatively, pack directly in convenient quantities in rigid containers. Remove the air, seal, label and freeze.

STORAGE TIME: 12 months

Dry-freezing, sweetened: Layer in rigid containers in convenient quantities with caster (superfine) sugar. Allow about 100 g/4 oz/½ cup sugar to every 450 g/1 lb fruit.

STORAGE TIME: 12 months

Purée-freezing: Purée the fruit in a blender or food processor, then pass through a sieve (strainer) to remove the seeds. Sweeten to taste, if liked, and pour in convenient quantities into rigid containers, leaving 2.5 cm/1 in headspace. Remove the air, seal, label and freeze.
STORAGE TIME: 12 months

To thaw and serve

Dry-frozen: Thaw at room temperature for about 2 hours, then use as required, or add frozen if making a hot dish.
Purée: Thaw at room temperature for 1–2 hours, then use, or heat from frozen in a saucepan or in the microwave.

Ratatouille

Ratatouille freezes beautifully.

To prepare

Cook in your usual way, but go easy on the garlic. Cool quickly.

To freeze

Pack in convenient quantities in rigid containers, leaving 2.5 cm/1 in headspace. Remove the air, seal, label and freeze.
STORAGE TIME: 6 months

To thaw and serve

To serve cold: Thaw overnight in the fridge or for several hours at room temperature, then serve as soon as possible after thawing.
To serve hot: Heat gently in a saucepan or cook in the microwave on Full Power until hot through, stirring gently and frequently.

Red beets   *See* **Beetroot**

Red cabbage   *See* **Cabbage**

Red kidney beans *See* **Beans, dried**

Red lentils *See* **Lentils**

Red mullet *See* **Mullet**

Redcurrants

Redcurrants are often used to make jelly (clear conserve). But if you have a glut, it's worth freezing them to add to fruit salads, pies, to use as a garnish or decoration or to make jelly at a later date. Select ripe fruit, still attached to their stalks. Avoid any that are mushy.

To prepare

Remove the fruit from their stalks by holding the stalk firmly and pulling it through the prongs of a fork. Wash and dry on kitchen paper (paper towels), if necessary.

To freeze

Dry-freezing: Spread out on baking (cookie) sheets and open-freeze until firm. Pack into rigid containers or polythene bags in convenient quantities. Remove the air, seal, label and store in the freezer.

STORAGE TIME: 12 months

Stew-freezing: Stew the fruit with 45–60 ml/3–4 tbsp water and 100–175 g/4–6 oz/½–¾ cup granulated sugar per 450 g/1 lb fruit, until the juice runs, but the fruit still holds its shape. Cool, then pack in rigid containers. Remove the air, seal, label and freeze.

STORAGE TIME: 12 months

To thaw and serve

Defrost at room temperature for 1–2 hours, then use as required. The fruit can be cooked from frozen for pies, fools etc.

Re-freezing

Most foods should not be re-frozen unless cooked first but there are a few exceptions, provided you are scrupulously hygienic. Follow these guidelines of what's safe and what's not.

YES:

* Food taken out of the freezer and placed in the fridge, then found not to be needed, can be returned and re-frozen provided ice crystals are still present in the food and it still feels very cold.
* Pastry (paste) that is thawed, rolled out and made into pies etc. can be re-frozen immediately without being cooked first. Similarly, if you need only half a pack of shortcrust (basic pie crust) or puff pastry, or just a few sheets of filo, the pack can be thawed, the amount needed selected and the remainder put back in the freezer.
* Bread can be removed and thawed enough to remove what's needed, then the remainder returned to the freezer.
* Cream can be thawed, whipped, then piped to decorate a dessert or to use in a dessert to be frozen, then returned to the freezer. Do work as quickly as possible though.
* Raw food can be thawed, then cooked, and re-frozen as a made-up dish.

NO:

* Never thaw cooked meats, poultry, pâtés or made-up meat or poultry dishes and re-freeze without cooking.
* Don't use frozen fish or shellfish or frozen cooked meats or poultry in an uncooked dish, then return it to the freezer – e.g. a mousse or in sandwiches.
* Don't freeze a made-up dish made with leftover ready-cooked meat, e.g. shepherd's pie made with cooked, minced (ground) lamb.
* Don't thaw foods at room temperature, leave them lying around, then decide to re-freeze them.

Reheating frozen food

Whether you reheat from frozen or once thawed, it is vital that food is piping hot throughout or bacteria will grow, causing food poisoning. This is particularly difficult to test with made-up dishes, like lasagne, pies, etc.

To make sure food is hot through, remove the dish from the oven or microwave. Insert a knife down through the centre of the food and wait 5 seconds. Remove the knife. The blade should feel burning hot. If not, reheat a little longer and test again.

Rhubarb

Select firm sticks with pink or green skin.

To prepare
Trim and cut into short lengths.

To freeze
Dry-freezing, unsweetened: Pack in convenient quantities in polythene bags. Remove the air, seal, label and freeze.
STORAGE TIME: 12 months

Syrup-freezing: Blanch the sticks in boiling water for 1 minute. Drain, plunge into a bowl of iced water to cool, then drain again. Pack in convenient quantities in rigid containers. Make a heavy syrup, using 350–450 g/ 12 oz–1 lb/1½–2 cups granulated sugar per 600 ml/1 pt/2½ cups water. Pour just enough over the fruit to cover, leaving 2.5 cm/1 in headspace. Remove the air, seal, label and freeze.
STORAGE TIME: 12 months

To thaw and serve
Thaw at room temperature for 1–2 hours, then use as required.

Rice, brown

To prepare
Cook in your usual way, following the packet directions. Drain, rinse with cold water, then drain thoroughly again. If freezing leftovers, make sure they are completely cold before freezing.

To freeze
Spoon the cooked rice in convenient quantities into a polythene bag or rigid container. Remove the air, seal, label and freeze.
STORAGE TIME: 6 months

To thaw and serve
If serving cold as a salad, thaw at room temperature for 2–3 hours or overnight in the fridge before adding the remaining ingredients. If serving hot, heat in boiling water or steam over a pan of boiling water for 4–5 minutes, stirring frequently to break up and heat evenly. Alternatively, heat in a covered container in the oven or microwave, stirring frequently. Make sure it is piping hot before serving.

Rice, long-grain

To prepare
Cook in your usual way, following packet directions. Drain, rinse with cold water, then drain thoroughly again. If freezing leftovers, make sure they are completely cold, too, before freezing.

To freeze
Spoon the cooked rice in convenient quantities into polythene bags or rigid containers. Remove the air, seal, label and freeze.

STORAGE TIME: 6 months

To thaw and serve
To serve cold: Thaw at room temperature for 2–3 hours or overnight in the fridge before adding the remaining ingredients.

To serve hot: Heat in boiling water for 4–5 minutes or steam over a pan of boiling water for the same amount of time, stirring frequently to break up and heat evenly. Alternatively, heat in a covered container in the oven or microwave, again, stirring frequently. Make sure the rice is hot right through before serving.

Rice pudding *See* **Milk puddings**

Rock salmon *See* **Huss**

Rolls *See* **Bread** *and* **Bread rolls, home-made**

Rosemary *See* **Herbs**

Rowanberries

These are best made into a jelly (clear conserve) but can be frozen to make into jelly later if you don't have the time when they are in season. Freeze when freshly picked.

To prepare

Pick preferably on a dry day. Rinse the bunches under cold, running water and pat dry on kitchen paper (paper towels). Strip the berries off the stalks using the prongs of a fork.

To freeze

Spread the berries in a single layer on a baking (cookie sheet). Open-freeze until firm. Tip into polythene bags or rigid containers. Remove the air, seal, label and freeze.

STORAGE TIME: 12 months

To thaw and serve

Thaw at room temperature for 1–2 hours, then use as required.

Runner beans *See* **Beans, runner**

Rutabaga *See* **Swede**

S

Sage   *See* **Herbs**

Saithe   *See* **Coley**

Salami   *See* **Delicatessen meats**

Salmon

Check with your fishmonger that the fish has not been previously frozen. The flesh should be firm and pink or orange with a fresh smell. If whole, the eyes and gills should be bright and the skin silvery.

To prepare

Whole fish must be cleaned. They can then be left whole or the head and tail removed, split open and boned. Alternatively, cut into steaks at the head end and fillets at the tail end. Rinse with cold water and pat dry on kitchen paper (paper towels).

To freeze

Whole: If freezing a prize whole fish for a special occasion, it is a good idea to ice-glaze it to preserve its appearance. Lay on foil and open-freeze on 'fast freeze' until firm. Dip the fish in cold water and open-freeze again until iced. Keep repeating this process until the glaze is about 5 mm/¼ in thick. Wrap tightly in clingfilm (plastic wrap), then firmly in foil, label and freeze.

Alternatively, simply wrap the whole fish tightly in clingfilm, then foil or a polythene bag. Remove the air, seal, label and freeze.

STORAGE TIME: 3 months

Fillets and steaks: Interleave with polythene interleave sheets or clingfilm, then pack in polythene bags, remove the air, seal, label and freeze.

STORAGE TIME: 3 months

To thaw and serve

Whole: Thaw whole fish in its wrappers in the fridge overnight. Place it on a large platter if ice-glazed, to collect the drips, then cook in your normal way.

Fillets and steaks: Thaw at room temperature for 1–2 hours, separating the fillets or steaks as soon as possible, then cook. Alternatively, cook from frozen, allowing 3–5 minutes' extra cooking time.

Salmon, smoked

Vacuum packs are best for freezing.

To prepare and freeze

If unopened, label and freeze, as it is. If the packet has been opened, wrap in clingfilm (plastic wrap), then tightly in foil. Label and freeze.

STORAGE TIME: 2 months

To thaw and serve

Defrost in its wrapper overnight in the fridge or for 2–3 hours at room temperature, then use as soon as possible.

Salsify

This long, white root freezes well. Choose young, firm roots.

To prepare

Scrub but do not peel or cut up. Blanch whole in boiling water for 3 minutes. Drain, then plunge in a bowl of iced water and cool. Drain and dry on kitchen paper (paper towels), then peel and cut into thick matchsticks.

To freeze

Pack in convenient quantities in polythene bags. Remove the air, seal, label and freeze.

STORAGE TIME: 12 months

To thaw and serve

Cook from frozen in boiling, lightly salted water for about 6 minutes. Drain and serve tossed in butter or in a white sauce.

Sandwiches

If your family all need packed lunches or you have a party coming up, make and freeze batches of sandwiches to save time and last-minute effort. Sandwiches frozen in the morning will be thawed by lunchtime and will, in fact, have kept better than if already at room temperature when packed!

Avoid fillings with foods that don't freeze well – hard-boiled (hard-cooked) eggs, mayonnaise and salad stuffs. Also don't use thawed frozen prawns (shrimp) or other shellfish, as these must not be re-frozen. Canned and fresh ones are fine.

To prepare
Make in your usual way.

To freeze
Wrap rounds individually in clingfilm (plastic wrap) or foil, then pack in a rigid container or larger bag for easier storage. Alternatively, wrap stacks of the same filling, interleaved with polythene interleave sheets or foil, then place in a polythene bag. Remove the air, seal, label and freeze.
STORAGE TIME: Meat filling 3 months, others 6 months

To thaw and serve
Thaw overnight in the fridge or at room temperature for about 2 hours, depending on the filling.

Satsumas

The satsuma season used to be short, so it was a treat to freeze them to have them out of season. Now, it's still worth freezing them ready for a quick fruit salad or when they are particularly cheap. Select sweet-smelling fruit that have firm skins and that feel heavy for their size. Those that are light or have loose skins may be dry.

To prepare
Peel, remove all the pith and divide into segments.

To freeze
Dry-freezing, sweetened: Pack in rigid containers in convenient quantities. Sprinkle each layer with 15–30 ml/1–2 tbsp granulated sugar. Remove the air, seal, label and freeze.
STORAGE TIME: 12 months

Syrup-freezing: Make a heavy sugar syrup using 350 g/12 oz/1½ cups granulated sugar to every 600 ml/1 pt/2½ cups water. Pack the segments in convenient quantities in rigid containers. Pour over the syrup to cover completely. Remove the air, seal, label and freeze.

STORAGE TIME: 12 months

To thaw and serve

Thaw at room temperature for 2–3 hours. Serve with breakfast cereal or ice cream, as part of a fruit salad or in a trifle.

Sauces

Any variety of sauces, from Bolognese to Velouté, can be frozen but there are a few things to remember.

* Sauces thickened with cornflour (cornstarch) – and even sometimes with flour – may separate on thawing. To rectify, give a good whisk with a wire or balloon whisk during reheating.
* Don't freeze egg-based sauces, such as Hollandaise or mayonnaise, as they will curdle when thawed.
* If adding cream or eggs for richness, add after thawing and reheating.
* It's worth making double the quantity when you make a sauce, then freezing half for a later date.

To prepare

Make in your usual way, but go easy on flavourings. You can always add extra when thawed. Cool quickly.

To freeze

Pour into rigid containers in convenient quantities, leaving 2.5 cm/1 in headspace. Remove the air, seal, label and freeze.

STORAGE TIME: 3 months

To thaw and serve

Thaw in the fridge overnight, at room temperature for 2–4 hours (depending on the density) or heat from frozen in a saucepan, stirring all the time until melted, then heat until piping hot.

Sausage rolls

You can buy ready-cooked fresh rolls or packs of ready-to-cook frozen rolls, but you can also make your own. If you are going to freeze the rolls raw, use fresh sausagemeat only, not thawed frozen.

To prepare
Make the rolls and cut into the size required. Leave raw or cook, as preferred.

To freeze
Raw: Place on non-stick baking parchment on baking (cookie) sheets. Open-freeze until firm. Pack in polythene bags. Remove the air, seal, label and freeze.

STORAGE TIME: 2 months

Cooked: Pack in polythene bags or rigid containers. Remove the air, seal, label and freeze.

STORAGE TIME: 3 months

To thaw and serve
Raw: Cook from frozen on baking (cookie) sheets in a preheated oven at 220°C/425°F/gas mark 7 (fan oven 200°C) for about 30 minutes until golden brown and cooked through.

Cooked: Reheat as above for about 15 minutes, covering loosely with foil if over-browning.

Sausagemeat

Sausagemeat can be bought frozen in packs that can be placed directly in your freezer. If you buy fresh, freeze as follows.

To prepare
Separate into convenient quantities. Leave whole or shape into small balls.

To freeze
Pack in convenient quantities in polythene bags. Pack balls in a rigid container. Remove the air, seal, label and freeze.

STORAGE TIME: 2 months

To thaw and serve
Thaw overnight in the fridge or for 2–4 hours (depending on the quantity) at room temperature and cook as soon as possible after thawing.

Sausages

Sausages freeze well but only for a short time because of their high fat content.

To prepare
If bought loose from your butcher, separate the links so they can be taken out of the freezer separately if required. If ready-wrapped, don't bother!

To freeze
Individual: If the links have been cut, interleave each sausage with polythene interleave sheets, foil or non-stick baking parchment, then wrap in clingfilm (plastic wrap), then foil, or place in a polythene bag.

Packs: Overwrap wrapped packs of sausages in a polythene bag for protection. Remove the air, seal, label and freeze.

STORAGE TIME: 2 months, 1 month if highly spiced

To thaw and serve
Thaw overnight in the fridge or for 2–3 hours at room temperature, then cook as usual, or cook from frozen, allowing a few minutes' extra time.

Scallops

Scallops can be frozen but only if they are very fresh, still in their shells. If they are already shelled, they will probably have been previously frozen – in which case, don't freeze.

To prepare
Lever the two halves of the shell apart. Cut the scallop out of the shell. Peel off the membrane that covers the fish and rinse under cold water. Drain on kitchen paper (paper towels). Scrub the deep shells and reserve for serving, if liked.

To freeze
Arrange in a single layer on a baking (cookie) sheet and freeze until firm. Pack in polythene bags or a rigid container; remove the air, seal, label and freeze.

STORAGE TIME: 1 month

To thaw and serve
Thaw overnight in the fridge or at room temperature for about 2 hours, then cook in your usual way.

Scampi

Scampi can be bought fresh or frozen, raw or cooked, shelled or unshelled. If fresh, check with your fishmonger that they have not been previously frozen. They are also sold breaded, ready to deep-fry.

Scampi should be firm and plump, and smell sweet and pleasantly fishy.

To prepare
Rinse under cold water and pat dry on kitchen paper (paper towels).

To freeze
Pack in convenient quantities in polythene bags or rigid containers. Remove the air, seal, label and freeze.
STORAGE TIME: 1 month

To thaw and serve
Cooked: Thaw in the fridge overnight or at room temperature for 1–2 hours, then use immediately. They can be added from frozen to cooked dishes, but they will add a quantity of liquid to the finished dish as they thaw.
Raw: Cook from frozen in your usual way.

Scones (biscuits)

Scones freeze well, but are at their best straight from the oven!

To prepare
Make and cook in your usual way. Cool on a wire rack.

To freeze
Pack in polythene bags. Remove the air, seal, label and freeze.
STORAGE TIME: 6 months

To thaw and serve
Thaw at room temperature for 2–3 hours, then, if liked, wrap in foil and warm in the oven at 180°C/350°F/gas mark 4 (fan oven 160°C) for about 5 minutes. Alternatively, place on kitchen paper (paper towels) in the microwave and warm on Full Power for about 15–20 seconds per scone.

Scorzonera

This long, black-skinned root freezes well. Choose young, firm roots.

To prepare
Scrub but do not peel or cut up.

To freeze
Blanch in boiling water for 3 minutes. Drain and plunge in a bowl of iced water and leave to cool. Drain and dry on kitchen paper (paper towels), then peel and cut into thick matchsticks. Pack in convenient quantities in polythene bags. Remove the air, seal, label and freeze.
STORAGE TIME: 12 months

To thaw and serve
Cook from frozen in boiling, lightly salted water for about 6 minutes. Drain and serve tossed in butter or in a white sauce.

Sealing
All packages must be sealed and the air excluded before they are placed in the freezer. This can be done in two ways.
* Using rigid plastic containers with tight-sealing lids: put on the lids, then lift up at one corner. Squeeze out the air, then snap the lid shut.
* Using polythene bags: half-close the neck, suck out the air with a straw or squeeze it out with your hands, then seal the bag using twist ties, rubber bands, bag clips or a special heat-sealing machine. (This last is not likely unless you are a serious freezer fan, although you can improvise using your iron on the lowest setting, protecting the iron by laying the ends of the polythene bag between two sheets of non-stick baking parchment).

Serrano ham *See* **Ham, raw, cured**

Seville oranges

You can freeze Seville oranges when they are in season to make into marmalade at other times of the year. Select fruit that feel heavy for their size. They will all be misshapen but this doesn't matter.

To prepare

Wash the whole fruit and dry on kitchen paper (paper towels).

To freeze

Pack whole in polythene bags. Remove the air, seal, label and freeze.
STORAGE TIME: 12 months

To thaw and serve

Thaw at room temperature for 2–3 hours before preparing. Use a recipe that calls for whole fruit.

Shellfish   *See individual entries, e.g.* **Scallops**

Shepherd's pie

This method applies also to Cottage pie. The only difference is that Shepherd's pie is made with lamb, and Cottage pie with beef.

Freeze only if made with fresh meat, not cooked leftover meat from the Sunday joint.

To prepare

Make up the dish in your usual way but do not bake. Leave to cool.

To freeze

Open-freeze until firm, then wrap firmly in foil, label and return to the freezer.
STORAGE TIME: 3 months

To thaw and serve

Unwrap. Cook from frozen in a preheated oven at 190°C/375°F/gas mark 5 (fan oven 170°C) for about 1 hour until piping hot and golden brown on top.

Shortbread

Shortbread is really useful to have ready to serve with desserts or a cup of tea or coffee.

To prepare

Make and bake in your usual way. Partially cool in the tin (pan), then transfer to a wire rack to cool completely.

To freeze

Wrap in foil or pack in a rigid container. Remove the air, seal, label and freeze.

STORAGE TIME: 6 months

To thaw and serve

Leave wrapped at room temperature for about 1 hour to thaw completely.

Shortcrust pastry (basic pie crust)

A ball of raw pastry (paste) takes several hours to thaw at room temperature but can be defrosted quickly in the microwave. Ideally, roll it out into lids and cases (shells), and freeze, ready to fill and bake from frozen.

To prepare

For freezing raw: Make the pastry in your usual way. Roll out and cut into large and small rounds. Cut some oval ones to fit particular pie dishes, if liked, or use to line flan rings, set on baking (cookie) sheets, or foil pie dishes and tartlet tins (patty pans).

For freezing cooked: Prepare flan or tartlet cases as above but bake blind in your usual way.

To freeze

Lids, raw: Place rounds or ovals on baking sheets. Make a small steam-hole in the centre. Open-freeze until firm. Pack lids together, interleaved with polythene interleave sheets, non-stick baking parchment or foil, in a rigid container. Remove the air, seal, label and return to the freezer.

STORAGE TIME: 6 months

Cases, large and small, raw: Open-freeze until firm. Remove flan cases from flan rings, wrap in foil, then pack in rigid containers to protect them. Remove tartlet cases from the tin, wrap in foil, then pack in a rigid container for protection. Remove the air, seal, label and return to the freezer.

STORAGE TIME: 6 months

Cooked: Cool, wrap in foil or polythene bags, then place in rigid containers for protection. Remove the air, seal, label and freeze.

STORAGE TIME: 6 months

To thaw and serve

Lids, raw: Prepare the dish to be covered. Dampen the edge with water and place the pastry lid in position. Bake in a preheated oven at 200°C/400°F/gas mark 6 (fan oven 180°C) for 20–25 minutes, then turn down the heat to 180°C/350°F/gas mark 4 (fan oven 160°C) for a further 15–20 minutes until golden and cooked through.

Cases, large, raw: Return the case to the ring on a baking sheet or place in a serving dish. Bake blind from frozen in a preheated oven at 200°C/400°F/gas mark 6 (fan oven 180°C) for 20–25 minutes until crisp and golden, then use as required, or fill, then bake open as above for about 30–35 minutes. Alternatively, fill, dampen the edge, cover with a frozen pastry lid and bake as above for 20–25 minutes, then turn down the temperature to 180°C/350°F/gas mark 4 (fan oven 160°C) for a further 15–20 minutes or until golden and cooked through.

Cases, small, raw: Return to the tartlet tin while frozen and bake blind as above but for about 15 minutes, or fill, brush the edges with water, top with lids and bake for about 20 minutes until golden and cooked through.

Cooked: Thaw at room temperature for 1–2 hours. Use as required.

Shortening *See* **Lard**

Shrimp *See* **Prawns**

Shrimps

Small brown or pink shrimps are delicious freshly harvested and boiled. They must be absolutely fresh for freezing. They are best bought whole, then peeled yourself (I'm afraid it's a time-consuming operation!). They should smell sweet and pleasantly fishy. Avoid if they smell of ammonia.

To prepare
Rinse under cold water and pat dry on kitchen paper (paper towels). If raw, boil in salted water for 3–4 minutes, then drain and cool quickly.

To freeze
Pull off the heads and tails and peel off the shell and legs. Pack in convenient quantities in polythene bags. Remove the air, seal, label and freeze.
STORAGE TIME: 1 month

To thaw and serve
Thaw in the fridge overnight or at room temperature for 1–2 hours, then use immediately. They can be added from frozen to cooked dishes.

Shrimps, potted

To prepare
Make up the recipe in your usual way in individual pots.

To freeze
Cover tightly in clingfilm (plastic wrap), then in foil. Label and freeze.
STORAGE TIME: 1 month

To thaw and serve
Ideally, thaw in the fridge overnight. They may be thawed at room temperature for 2–3 hours, then served immediately.

Skate wings

Check with your fishmonger that the fish has not been previously frozen. The flesh should be firm and white, the bones opaque, and it should smell fresh.

To prepare
Rinse with cold water and pat dry on kitchen paper (paper towels).

To freeze
Interleave with polythene interleave sheets or clingfilm (plastic wrap), then pack in polythene bags, remove the air, seal, label and freeze.
STORAGE TIME: 3 months

To thaw and serve
Thaw at room temperature for 2 hours first, separating the wings as soon as possible, or cook from frozen, allowing 3–5 minutes' extra cooking time.

Slicing sausage See **Delicatessen meats**

Smoked foods See individual entries, e.g. **Salmon, smoked**

Snipe
Choose plump birds, allowing one per person.

To prepare
They are usually sold undrawn, and traditionally the head is left on and tucked underneath so the long beak holds the bird in shape. Clean them and remove the head if you prefer before freezing, and put the heart, gizzard and liver in a small polythene bag to freeze separately from the bird. Rinse inside and out with cold water and pat dry on kitchen paper (paper towels). Truss.

To freeze
Protect the bone ends with foil, then pack in a polythene bag with the bag of giblets. Remove the air, seal, label and freeze.
STORAGE TIME: Cleaned birds 6 months, giblets and undrawn birds 3 months

To thaw and serve
Thaw in the fridge for up to 24 hours and cook as soon as defrosted.

Snow peas See **Mangetout**

Soda bread

Soda bread freezes well.

To prepare
Make and cook in your usual way. Cool, then split into quarters.

To freeze
Pack in polythene bags. Remove the air, seal, label and freeze.
STORAGE TIME: 6 months

To thaw and serve
Thaw at room temperature for 2 hours or heat from frozen in a preheated oven at 200°C/400°F/gas mark 6 (fan oven 180°C) for about 10 minutes.

Sole

Dover sole and lemon sole are the two most popular varieties. Check with your fishmonger that the fish has not been previously frozen. The flesh should be firm with a fresh smell. If whole, the eyes should be bright.

To prepare
Rinse with cold water and pat dry on kitchen paper (paper towels). Whole fish may be filleted.

To freeze
Interleave with polythene interleave sheets or clingfilm (plastic wrap), then pack in polythene bags, remove the air, seal, label and freeze.
STORAGE TIME: 3 months

To thaw and serve
Trim the fins and tails of whole fish. Cook from frozen, in your usual way, allowing 3–5 minutes' extra cooking time, or thaw at room temperature for 2 hours first.

Sorbets

The important thing about making your own sorbets is to whisk well several times during freezing. The egg whites should be folded in very gently when the sorbet is half-frozen, and whisked to a mush. Ready-made sorbets should, of course, be transferred to your freezer as soon as possible after buying.

To prepare
Make up the fruit mixture in your usual way.

To freeze
Turn the sorbet mixture into a rigid container and freeze for about 2 hours until frozen round the edges. Whisk with a fork to break up the ice crystals, then freeze again for a further 2 hours. Whisk well again, then fold in the whisked egg whites. Freeze again until firm.

STORAGE TIME: 3 months

To thaw and serve
Remove from the freezer about 15 minutes before serving to soften slightly. Replace in the freezer as soon as you've spooned out the amount to be served.

Soufflés, cold

To prepare
Prepare the soufflé dish using foil instead of greaseproof (waxed) paper to make the collar. Join it with freezer tape or an elastic band and a paper clip at the top. Make the soufflé in your usual way and turn into the dish. Do not decorate.

To freeze
Open-freeze until firm, then wrap in a polythene bag. Remove the air, seal, label and return to the freezer.

STORAGE TIME: 3 months

To thaw and serve
Remove the bag and then carefully remove the collar while still frozen and decorate. Thaw in the fridge overnight or at room temperature for 3–4 hours.

Soufflés, hot

To prepare
Make in your usual way, but do not add the egg whites.

To freeze
Spoon into a rigid container, remove the air, seal, label and freeze.
STORAGE TIME: 3 months

To thaw and serve
Thaw the mixture at room temperature for 2 hours. Whisk the egg whites until stiff and fold into the mixture with a metal spoon. Turn into a prepared soufflé dish and bake in your usual way.

Soups

To prepare
Make in your usual way, but use only a little seasoning and flavouring as freezing may alter their strength. You can adjust them when reheating after thawing. Cool quickly. If the recipe calls for cream or egg yolks, leave these out, to be added after thawing and reheating.

To freeze
Pour into a rigid container, leaving 2.5 cm/1 in headspace. Remove the air, seal, label and freeze.
STORAGE TIME: 3 months

To thaw and serve
Reheat from frozen in a saucepan or in the microwave on Full Power, breaking up the block and stirring frequently until piping hot throughout. Alternatively, defrost at room temperature for about 3 hours, then reheat. Taste and re-season, and add cream or egg yolks, if necessary.

Soused herrings   *See* **Herrings, soused**

Soya beans   *See* **Beans, dried**

Spaghetti   *See* **Pasta**

Spinach

Spinach freezes well. Select young leaves. Large, old, fibrous ones will have a strong taste and may be stringy. Avoid any yellowing or damaged leaves.

To prepare

Remove any tough stalks; wash the spinach well in cold, running water, then drain. Blanch in boiling water for 1 minute, then drain and plunge immediately in a bowl of iced water to cool. Drain and squeeze out as much moisture as possible with a spoon. Snip with scissors, if liked, to chop, or leave whole.

To freeze

Pack in convenient quantities in polythene bags. Remove the air, seal, label and freeze.

STORAGE TIME: 12 months

To thaw and serve

Cook from frozen in a covered saucepan without any extra water for about 5 minutes, stirring occasionally until piping hot. Drain off any liquid; season with salt, pepper and nutmeg, then stir in some cream, if liked.

Sponge cakes *See* **Cake, sponge** *and* **Batch baking**

Sprats

Sprats are small herring-like fish, ideal for frying (sautéing), grilling (broiling) and barbecuing. Select very fresh fish with bright eyes and gills and a pleasant smell. Check with your fishmonger that they have not been previously frozen.

To prepare

Clean and leave whole. Rinse with cold water and pat dry on kitchen paper (paper towels).

To freeze

Place in convenient quantities in polythene bags. Remove the air, seal, label and freeze.

STORAGE TIME: 2 months

To thaw and serve

Thaw fish just long enough to separate. Toss in seasoned flour, if liked, then cook in your usual way, allowing an extra 2 minutes' cooking time.

Spring (collard) greens

Select dark green leaves and avoid any with yellowing edges.

To prepare

Separate into leaves and remove the thick stalks; wash well in cold water and drain. Blanch the whole leaves in boiling water for 1 minute. Drain and plunge immediately in a bowl of iced water to cool. Drain again and dry on kitchen paper (paper towels) and shred.

To freeze

Pack in convenient quantities in polythene bags. Remove the air, seal, label and freeze.

STORAGE TIME: 6 months

To thaw and serve

Cook from frozen in boiling, lightly salted water for 6–8 minutes.

Sprouts *See* **Brussels sprouts**

Squab

Squab are small pigeons, bred for the table. Allow one per person.

To prepare

Pluck and draw, if necessary. Wash in cold water, then dry inside and out with kitchen paper (paper towels). If keeping the giblets, reserve the heart, liver, neck and gizzard and pack in a separate polythene bag.

To freeze

Protect the bone ends with foil, then pack in polythene bags. Add the bag of giblets. Remove the air, seal, label and freeze.

STORAGE TIME: Birds 6 months, giblets 3 months

To thaw and serve

Thaw in the fridge for up to 24 hours and cook as soon as defrosted.

Squash *See* **Marrow**

Steamed puddings

Steamed sponge and suet puddings freeze well.

To prepare

Prepare and cook in your usual way. Leave to cool.

To freeze

Remove the cooking papers and re-cover the basin with a double thickness of foil. Overwrap in a polythene bag. Remove the air, seal, label and freeze.

STORAGE TIME: 3 months

To thaw and serve

Remove the bag. Steam from frozen over a pan of hot water for about 45 minutes until piping hot throughout. Alternatively, heat in the microwave on Medium for about 8–10 minutes.

> See also **Christmas pudding**

Stem lettuce See **Chinese leaves**

Stews

Stews freeze well but avoid large pieces of potato, which may become watery when thawed. Dumplings should be lifted out of the stew and frozen separately (see Dumplings).

To prepare

Make in your usual way, but go easy on the seasoning. You can adjust this when reheating. Cool quickly.

To freeze

Pour into a rigid container, leaving 2.5 cm/1 in headspace. Remove the air, seal, label and freeze.

STORAGE TIME: 3 months

To thaw and serve

Thaw overnight in the fridge at room temperature for 3–4 hours, then reheat in a saucepan, stirring gently occasionally. Alternatively, defrost on Medium–low in the microwave, then reheat on Medium, stirring gently every minute or two until piping hot.

Tip: Push the solid ingredients in a stew or casserole down into the liquid before freezing, so there is a layer of liquid on top. This helps to protect against freezer burn.

Stir-fry vegetables

Vegetables frozen already cut into strips are ideal for a quick Oriental meal. You can buy packs ready-prepared (worth freezing if on special offer) or prepare your own as follows.

To prepare
Cut a variety of vegetables, such as courgettes (zucchini), carrots, (bell) peppers, etc., into matchsticks or shreds. Blanch the vegetables in boiling water for 1 minute. Plunge immediately in a bowl of iced water to cool. Drain and dry on kitchen paper (paper towels).

To freeze
Pack in convenient quantities in polythene bags. Remove the air, seal, label and freeze.

STORAGE TIME: 12 months

To thaw and serve
Cook from frozen using your normal recipe, adding on an extra 3–5 minutes' cooking time.

Stock

It's best to make concentrated stock for freezing as it takes up less space.

To prepare
Make in your usual way but then boil rapidly after cooking to reduce the liquid by half and concentrate the flavour. Strain and cool quickly.

To freeze
Pour in convenient quantities into rigid containers. Remove the air, seal, label and freeze.

STORAGE TIME: 3 months

To thaw and use
Heat from frozen in a saucepan or thaw at room temperature for about 2 hours before use.

Storage times

Storage times are important. Don't worry if you miss them by a day or two, but leaving foods in the freezer for longer may impair their texture and flavour. They won't, however, do you any harm – they just won't taste too good!

Strawberries

Select just ripe fruit. If over- or under-ripe, they won't freeze well.

To prepare

Pick over and remove any hulls. Wash and pat dry on kitchen paper (paper towels) only if absolutely necessary.

To freeze

Dry-freezing, unsweetened: Spread out on a baking (cookie) sheet. Open-freeze until firm, then pack in polythene bags or rigid containers. Remove the air, seal, label and freeze.
STORAGE TIME: 12 months

Dry-freezing, sweetened: Layer in rigid containers in convenient quantities with caster (superfine) sugar. Allow about 100 g/4 oz/½ cup sugar for every 450 g/1 lb fruit.
STORAGE TIME: 12 months

Purée-freezing: Purée the fruit in a blender or food processor or mash thoroughly with a fork. Sweeten to taste, if liked, and put in convenient quantities in rigid containers, leaving 2.5 cm/1 in headspace. Remove the air, seal, label and freeze.
STORAGE TIME: 12 months

To thaw and serve

Dry-frozen: Thaw at room temperature for about 2 hours, then use as required. They may be added frozen to a hot dish.

Purée: Thaw, then use, or heat from frozen in a saucepan or in the microwave.

Stuffings

Any stuffings can be prepared and frozen for use as required. They should not be frozen inside poultry or joints of meat.

To prepare
Make in your usual way.

To freeze
Pack in convenient quantities in polythene bags or rigid containers. Remove the air, seal, label and freeze.
STORAGE TIME: 3 months, on average (this will vary according to the ingredient with the shortest freezer life)

To thaw and serve
Thaw in the fridge overnight or at room temperature for about 2 hours, then use as required.

Suet

Animal or vegetable suet can be frozen but pre-packed suet has such a long shelf life it is hardly worth it. If you have a block of fresh animal suet, this is how to prepare it.

To prepare and freeze
Peel off the outer membrane, then dip the block in flour and coarsely grate, dipping in flour as you go to keep the shavings separate. Pack in convenient quantities in polythene bags. Remove the air, seal, label and freeze.
STORAGE TIME: 6 months

To thaw and use
Use from frozen.

Suet puddings   *See* **Steamed puddings**

Sugar snap peas

Sugar snap peas are cooked and eaten complete, with their pods. They freeze well and are useful to serve as a vegetable accompaniment or part of a stir-fry. Select crisp, bright green, plump pods. Avoid any that look greyish or shrivelled.

To prepare

Top and tail. Blanch in boiling water for 1 minute. Drain and plunge in a bowl of iced water to cool. Drain again and dry on kitchen paper (paper towels).

To freeze

Spread out on a baking (cookie) sheet and freeze until firm, then pack in polythene bags, or pack in convenient quantities in polythene bags. Remove the air, seal, label and freeze.

STORAGE TIME: 12 months

To thaw and serve

Cook from frozen in boiling, lightly salted water for 3–5 minutes until just tender but still with some bite. Alternatively, cook from frozen in a stir-fry.

Swede (rutabaga)

Select small or medium-sized specimens. Extra-large ones tend to be woody.

To prepare

Peel and cut into dice. Blanch in boiling water for 2 minutes. Plunge immediately in a bowl of iced water to cool. Drain and dry on kitchen paper (paper towels).

To freeze

Pack in convenient quantities in polythene bags or rigid containers.

To thaw and serve

Cook from frozen in boiling, lightly salted water for about 6–8 minutes until tender. Drain and serve tossed in butter, or mash with a little butter or cream and season with lots of freshly ground black pepper.

Sweet potatoes

To prepare
Peel and cut into dice or larger even-sized pieces. Blanch for 2 minutes in boiling water with 15 ml/1 tbsp lemon juice added. Drain and plunge immediately in a bowl of iced water to cool. Drain and dry on kitchen paper (paper towels).

To freeze
Pack in convenient quantities in polythene bags. Remove the air, seal, label and freeze.
STORAGE TIME: 12 months

To thaw and serve
Dice: Boil in lightly salted water for about 8 minutes until tender, then toss in butter or mash.
Larger pieces: Thaw at room temperature enough to separate, then toss in hot oil and roast for about 1 hour at the top of a preheated oven at 200°C/400°F/gas mark 6 (fan oven 180°C) until golden and tender.

Sweetcorn (corn) kernels
It's not worth taking the kernels off corn cobs to freeze when you can buy ready-prepared frozen corn kernels very reasonably.

See also **Corn on the cob**

Swiss chard

To prepare
Separate into leaves and remove the thick stalks. Wash the remaining stalks and leaves well in cold water and drain. Tie the stalks in a bundle. Blanch the stalks in boiling water for 2 minutes, the leaves for 1 minute. Drain and plunge immediately in a bowl of iced water to cool. Drain again and dry on kitchen paper. Shred the leaves.

To freeze
Leaves: Pack in convenient quantities in polythene bags. Remove the air, seal, label and freeze.
STORAGE TIME: 6 months

Stalks: Pack in a separate bag. Remove the air, seal, label and freeze.
STORAGE TIME: 6 months

To thaw and serve
Cook leaves and stalks separately from frozen in boiling, lightly salted water for 6–8 minutes.
Leaves: Serve as a vegetable accompaniment.
Stalks: Serve with melted butter as a starter, like asparagus.

Swiss (jelly) rolls
These freeze well. They should be rolled in cornflour (cornstarch) rather than caster (superfine) sugar before freezing and, ideally, frozen unfilled, then filled when thawed.

To prepare
Make in your usual way. Turn out on to a piece of non-stick baking parchment dusted with cornflour. Roll up.

To freeze
Overwrap in a polythene bag. Remove the air. Seal, label and freeze.
STORAGE TIME: 6 months

To thaw and serve
Thaw at room temperature for 2–3 hours. When completely thawed, carefully unroll, spread with your chosen filling, then re-roll.

Swordfish
Select even-sized thick steaks with moist flesh and a fresh smell. Check with your fishmonger that they have not been previously frozen.

To freeze
Wrap individually in clingfilm (plastic wrap), then in a polythene bag. Remove the air, seal, label and freeze.
STORAGE TIME: 3 months

To thaw and serve
Cook from frozen, allowing an extra 3–5 minutes' cooking time.

Syrup-freezing

This is a way of preserving fruits in syrup that can be used when serving the fruit. The strength depends on the acidity of the fruit. Most have a light (40 per cent) syrup, made with 225 g/8 oz/1 cup granulated sugar for every 600 ml/1 pt/2½ cups water. Some need a heavy (60–80 per cent) syrup, made with 350–450 g/12 oz–1 lb/1½–2 cups sugar for every 600 ml/1 pt/2½ cups water. This quantity will be enough for about 900 g/2 lb fruit.

See individual fruit entries for full details of freezing and storage times.

t

Tabbouleh

Tabbouleh can be prepared and frozen complete, but I prefer to add the diced cucumber and tomato on thawing to keep its texture.

To prepare

Cook the bulghar (cracked wheat) according to your usual recipe. Add all the remaining ingredients except the cucumber and tomato.

To freeze

Spoon in convenient quantities into polythene bags. Remove the air, seal, label and freeze.

STORAGE TIME: 6 months

To thaw and serve

Thaw overnight in the fridge or for 2 hours at room temperature, then add the finely diced cucumber and tomato and serve.

Tangerines

Tangerines are not as common now as clementines and satsumas so it's worth freezing them as their flavour is superior, in my opinion. Select sweet-smelling fruit that have firm skins and that feel heavy for their size. Those that are light or have loose skins may be dry.

To prepare

Peel, remove all the pith and segment. Remove any pips.

To freeze

Dry-freezing, sweetened: Pack in rigid containers in convenient quantities. Sprinkle each layer with 15–30 ml/1–2 tbsp granulated sugar. Remove the air, seal, label and freeze.

STORAGE TIME: 12 months

Syrup-freezing: Make a heavy sugar syrup using 350 g/12 oz/1½ cups granulated sugar for every 600 ml/1 pt/2½ cups water. Pack the segments in convenient quantities in rigid containers. Pour over the syrup to cover completely. Remove the air, seal, label and freeze.
STORAGE TIME: 12 months

To thaw and serve
Thaw at room temperature for 2–3 hours. Serve with breakfast cereals, as part of a fruit salad or in a trifle.

Taramasalata
Although you can freeze smoked cod's roe, this dip is best made fresh as it tends to separate on thawing.

Tarragon   See **Herbs**

Tarts
Tarts or open flans are best frozen after cooking. However, tartlet cases can be frozen separately, raw or cooked.

To prepare
Make large or small tarts and cook in your usual way, using a foil pie plate, if possible, or a flan ring, set on a baking (cookie) sheet. Make small tartlets in tartlet tins (patty pans) or individual foil dishes. Cool.

To freeze
Large: Wrap foil dishes in foil or a polythene bag. Open-freeze if made in a flan ring, then remove the ring. Remove the air, seal, label and freeze.
STORAGE TIME: 6 months
Small: Open-freeze tartlets in their tins, then take out of the tins and pack as before. Remove the air, seal, label and freeze.
STORAGE TIME: 6 months

To thaw and serve
To serve cold: Thaw at room temperature for 2–4 hours (depending on the filling).
To serve hot: If made in a flan ring, put the tart on a baking sheet and replace the ring. Reheat from frozen in a preheated oven at 180°C/350°F/gas mark 4 (fan oven 160°C) for about 30 minutes until piping hot. Small tartlets

can be returned to their tins or placed on a baking (cookie) sheet for reheating at the same temperature for about 10 minutes. Tarts in foil containers can be reheated and served in the same containers.

See also **Bakewell tart, Shortcrust pastry**

Teabreads

To prepare
Make in your usual way, remove from the tin (pan) and cool on a wire rack.

To freeze
Wrap in foil or a polythene bag. Slice first, if preferred. Remove the air, seal, label and freeze.
STORAGE TIME: 6 months

To thaw and serve
Whole: Thaw at room temperature for 3–4 hours.
Slices: Thaw for about 30 minutes or heat slices briefly from frozen in the toaster, under the grill (broiler) or in the microwave on Full Power for 15–20 seconds per slice. Spread with butter, if liked.

Teacakes

Teacakes, like all buns, freeze well.

To freeze
Place in polythene bags, remove the air, seal, label and freeze.
STORAGE TIME: 4 months

To thaw and serve
Thaw at room temperature in their bags for 2 hours or thaw in the microwave on Medium–low for a few seconds per bun, then reheat for a few seconds per bun on Full Power. Alternatively, wrap in foil and bake in a preheated oven at 200°C/400°F/gas mark 6 (fan oven 180°C) for 5–10 minutes until thawed and warm. If you have a serrated-edged knife, you can halve them while frozen and toast them.

Thyme   *See* **Herbs**

Tiger prawns (jumbo shrimp)   *See* **Prawns**

Toasted sandwiches

Sandwiches for toasting can be frozen ready for meals in a hurry.

To prepare

Make up the sandwiches in your usual way but with the buttered sides of the bread on the outside. Avoid fillings that don't freeze well, like hard-boiled (hard-cooked) eggs, mayonnaise and salad stuffs – sliced tomatoes will be all right in toasted sandwiches. Make sure the filling is evenly distributed and not too thick.

To freeze

Wrap in non-stick baking parchment, then foil. Label and freeze.

To thaw and serve

Upwrap and cook from frozen in a sandwich toaster, under the grill (broiler) or gently in a frying pan (skillet), allowing an extra 3–5 minutes' cooking time to allow for thawing in the centre.

Tofu

Tofu, or beancurd, does not freeze well.

Tomatoes

Tomatoes cannot be frozen, then served raw in salads, as their high water content makes them soft when thawed. But they can be frozen for use in cooked dishes, to fry (sauté) or grill (broil) and as juice, purée or a sauce. Select tomatoes that are ripe.

To prepare

Whole: Wash and remove the calyxes.
For juice or purée: Plunge into boiling water for 30 seconds, then peel off the skins. Chop roughly and purée in a blender or food processor. Tip into a saucepan and simmer for 5 minutes. Strain through a sieve (strainer). For purée, return to the saucepan and continue to cook for about 30 minutes, stirring frequently, to thicken it and evaporate the liquid, concentrating the flavour. Cool quickly.
For a sauce: Make in your usual way, then cool quickly.

To freeze

Whole: Pack in convenient quantities in polythene bags. Remove the air, seal, label and freeze.
STORAGE TIME: 12 months

Juice: Pour in convenient quantities into rigid containers, leaving 2.5 cm/1 in headspace. Remove the air, seal, label and freeze.
STORAGE TIME: 12 months
Purée: Pour into ice cube trays. Open-freeze until firm, then tip into polythene bags. Remove the air, seal, label and return to the freezer. Each cube will yield about 15 ml/1 tbsp purée.
STORAGE TIME: 12 months
Sauce: Pour into a rigid container, leaving 2.5 cm/1 in headspace. Remove the air, seal, label and freeze.
STORAGE TIME: 12 months

To thaw and serve
Whole: Thaw at room temperature for about 2 hours, then grill, fry or add to cooked dishes. They can be stewed from frozen, if preferred.
Juice: Thaw in the fridge for several hours or overnight. Serve very cold.
Purée: Use cubes from frozen to flavour savoury dishes.

Tortillas, flour
To prepare and freeze
Freeze in their vacuum packs. No preparation is needed.

To thaw and serve
Packs: Thaw packs at room temperature for about 1 hour.
Individual: Thaw the pack briefly, remove one tortilla, wrap in kitchen paper (paper towels) and microwave for a few seconds on Full Power.

Trout
Trout are now farmed so are available all the year round. It's worth freezing them when you find them on special offer or if you are lucky enough to have some freshly caught. Select fish with shiny skin, bright eyes and gills and a pleasant smell.

To prepare
Clean and leave whole, or fillet. Rinse with cold water and pat dry on kitchen paper (paper towels).

To freeze
Wrap whole fish or fillets individually in clingfilm (plastic wrap), then place in a polythene bag. Remove the air, seal, label and freeze.
STORAGE TIME: 2 months

To thaw and serve

Thaw whole fish just long enough to allow you to make several slashes on each side. Cook in your usual way, allowing an extra 3–5 minutes' cooking time. Cook fillets from frozen, again adding extra cooking time.

Turbot

Turbot is a very superior flat fish. It can only be frozen at home if very fresh. Check with your fishmonger that it has not been previously frozen. A whole fish can be enormous so you will probably buy fillets. Smaller 'chicken' turbot are available, weighing around 3 kg/6 lb.

To prepare

Cut into fillets, if necessary; leave chicken turbot whole. Rinse with cold water and pat dry on kitchen paper (paper towels).

To freeze

Fillets: Interleave with polythene interleave sheets or clingfilm (plastic wrap). Pack in polythene bags, remove the air, seal, label and freeze.
STORAGE TIME: 3 months
Whole fish: Wrap in clingfilm, then pack in polythene bags. Remove the air, seal, label and freeze.
STORAGE TIME: 3 months

To thaw and serve

Fillets: Thaw at room temperature for 2 hours, separating as soon as possible, then cook in your usual way. Alternatively cook from frozen, allowing 3–5 minutes' extra cooking time.
Whole fish: Thaw in the fridge overnight, then cook in your usual way.

Turkey

Look out for fresh turkeys on special offer. Christmas Eve or Easter Saturday afternoon are the prime times for super savers!

To prepare

Draw or pluck if necessary, reserving the neck, gizzard, heart and liver and discarding the remaining entrails. Ready-prepared turkeys need no further preparation. Do not stuff.

To freeze

Ready-wrapped: Overwrap in a polythene bag, remove the air, seal, label and freeze.

STORAGE TIME: Birds 9 months, giblets 3 months

Unwrapped: Cover the bone ends with foil, then wrap in a polythene bag, remove the air, seal, label and freeze.

STORAGE TIME: Birds 9 months, giblets 3 months

Portions: Freeze in their wrappings from the supermarket. If the packaging is thin, overwrap in a polythene bag for extra protection.

STORAGE TIME: 9 months

To thaw and serve

Whole birds: Thaw at room temperature for 1–3 days, depending on the size. Thaw any giblets in the fridge. Cook the bird as soon as it is thawed or put it in the fridge when nearly thawed until ready to cook. Don't leave standing at room temperature.

Portions and pieces: Thaw overnight in the fridge or at room temperature for 2–5 hours, depending on the thickness, then cook in your usual way. Diced turkey meat can be cooked from frozen, as long as you brown it first, breaking it up as you cook until every piece is separate and no longer pink, before adding the remaining ingredients.

Turkey, cooked meat

Freezing is particularly useful if you don't eat all the bird at Christmas.

To prepare

Pick off all the meat from the bones. The carcass can be used for stock (see separate entry).

To freeze

Wrap in convenient portions in foil, then polythene bags. Remove the air, seal, label and freeze.

STORAGE TIME: 3 months

To thaw and serve

Thaw in the fridge overnight or at room temperature for 2–3 hours. Serve cold or use in a cooked dish such as a pie, or a rice or pasta dish.

Turnips

Select small or medium-sized specimens. Extra-large ones tend to be woody.

To prepare

Peel and leave small ones whole, cut larger ones into dice. Blanch in boiling water for 2 minutes. Plunge immediately in a bowl of iced water to cool. Drain and dry on kitchen paper (paper towels).

To freeze

Pack in convenient quantities in polythene bags. Remove the air, seal, label and freeze.

STORAGE TIME: 12 months

To thaw and serve

Cook from frozen in boiling, lightly salted water for about 6–8 minutes until tender. Drain and serve tossed in butter or mash with a little butter or cream and season with lots of freshly ground black pepper.

U

Ugli fruit
Select fresh-smelling fruit that feel heavy for their size.

To prepare
Halve and squeeze the juice or peel, remove the pith and separate into segments.

To freeze
Juice: Pour into ice cube trays. Freeze, then pack in polythene bags. Remove the air, seal, label and freeze.
STORAGE TIME: 12 months
Segments, dry-freezing, sweetened: Pack the segments in convenient quantities in rigid containers, layering with caster (superfine) sugar, using about 225 g/8 oz/1 cup sugar for every 450 g/1 lb fruit.
STORAGE TIME: 12 months

To thaw and serve
Juice: Put cubes in glasses or a jug and thaw in the fridge overnight or at room temperature for 1–2 hours.
Segments: Thaw in the container at room temperature for 2–3 hours.

Upside-down pudding
This popular pudding freezes well.

To prepare
Make in your usual way, using pineapple, apricots or pears, but line the dish with oiled foil. Bake, then cool.

To freeze
Open-freeze until firm, then carefully remove the dish. Wrap in foil, label and return to the freezer.
STORAGE TIME: 3 months

To thaw and serve

Thaw at room temperature for 3–4 hours. Leave the foil base wrapping in place and reheat in a moderate oven for about 20 minutes until hot through. Remove the foil and serve.

Veal

Veal is rarely cheap and you are unlikely to buy it in bulk but there are bargains to be found.

To prepare

Pre-packed and labelled: No further preparation is necessary. Simply code and date.

Unwrapped: Trim stewing or braising meat and cut into dice if preferred, ready to casserole or stew. Leave in portion-sized slices if you prefer. Trim steaks and escalopes, if necessary. Separate into usable portions.

Joints: Do not stuff boned and rolled joints before freezing. Do this when you thaw the meat before roasting.

Minced (ground) veal: Shape into burgers or meatballs before freezing, if liked, or leave in useable portions for mince-based dishes.

To freeze

Joints and steaks: Cover any bone ends with foil first for extra protection, then pack in polythene bags. Remove the air, seal, label and freeze.
STORAGE TIME: 12 months

Burgers and meatballs: Pack in a rigid container, interleaved with non-stick baking parchment or clingfilm (plastic wrap) to prevent them sticking together. Remove the air, seal, label and freeze.
STORAGE TIME: 3 months

To thaw and serve

Ideally, thaw in the fridge for 5–6 hours per 450 g/1 lb or overnight. You can leave it in its wrapper and there will be little or no blood loss. It is, of course quicker to thaw at room temperature for 2–4 hours per 450 g/1 lb. Alternatively, use your microwave on Auto-defrost or Medium–low as follows:

Joints: Don't try to defrost joints completely in the microwave or they will start to cook before they thaw. Start them in the microwave, then finish at room temperature (see your manual for further details).

Cubes, steaks and escalopes: Separate as soon as possible during thawing in the microwave.

Minced veal: Scrape mince from the block as soon as it begins to thaw and remove from the microwave so it doesn't begin to cook.

Once thawed, cook in your usual way. Alternatively, minced or diced casserole or stewing veal can be cooked from frozen. Break up the lump of mince or cubes as soon as possible during cooking and keep stirring until no longer pink and all the grains or cubes are separate before adding other ingredients.

Vegetables, general principles for freezing

* Choose young, fresh vegetables for freezing. Old specimens will give tough, unpalatable results.
* Blanching is essential for most vegetables to prevent enzyme reaction. Plunge the prepared vegetables in boiling water, bring back to the boil and boil for 1–3 minutes (see individual entries).
* Rapid cooling is also vital. Drain the blanched vegetables and immediately plunge into iced water to prevent further cooking. This also helps retain their bright colour.
* Once cooled, drain thoroughly before freezing. This is usually done in a colander, then on kitchen paper (paper towels).
* Always pack vegetables for freezing in convenient quantities – small bags are usually best. You can always use two!

See also individual entries, e.g. **Beans, Peas**

Venison

To prepare
Check the venison has been hung (it needs at least a week before freezing to ensure its tenderness and flavour). If bought ready-wrapped from the supermarket, no further preparation is necessary: simply code and date.

To freeze
Wrap in polythene bags. Remove the air, seal, label and freeze.
STORAGE TIME: Joints 12 months, steaks and cubes 8 months, minced (ground) meat and sausages 3 months

To thaw and serve
Ideally, thaw in the fridge for 5–6 hours per 450 g/1 lb or overnight. You can leave it in its wrapper and there will be little or no blood loss. It is, of course quicker to thaw at room temperature for 2–4 hours per 450 g/1 lb.

Alternatively, use your microwave on Auto-defrost or Medium–low, using the following guidelines.

Joints: Don't try to defrost joints completely in the microwave or they will start to cook before they thaw. Start them in the microwave, then finish at room temperature (see your manual for further details).

Cubes, steaks and escalopes: Separate as soon as possible during thawing in the microwave.

Minced (ground) venison: Scrape mince from the block as soon as it begins to thaw and remove from the microwave so it doesn't begin to cook. Once thawed, cook in your usual way.

Minced and diced venison can also be cooked from frozen. Break up the lump of mince or cubes as soon as possible during cooking and keep stirring until it is no longer pink and all the grains or cubes are separate before adding other ingredients.

See also **Casseroles**

Victoria sandwich *See* **Cakes, sponge,** *and* **Batch baking**

Vol-au-vents

These little pastry cases (pie shells) can be frozen raw or cooked but are best filled after thawing.

To prepare
Make up the pastry (paste) and cut to size in your usual way.

To freeze
Raw: Transfer to baking (cookie) sheets. Open-freeze until firm. Pack in polythene bags or rigid containers. Remove the air, seal, label and freeze.
STORAGE TIME: 6 months
Cooked: Bake in your usual way. Cool. Pack in rigid containers as they are very fragile. Remove the air, seal, label and freeze.
STORAGE TIME: 6 months

To thaw and serve
Raw: Put on a dampened baking sheet. Bake in a preheated oven at 230°C/450°F/gas mark 8 (fan oven 210°C) for about 15 minutes until risen and golden.
Cooked: Bake in the same way but for only about 5 minutes until hot through and crisp. Fill hot or cold and use as required.

Water

Yes, water can be frozen! Seriously, it's worth keeping a stock of ice cubes, especially if you are going to be freezing lots of vegetables as you'll need plenty of ice for the blanching process. And if you like lots of gin and tonics ...

To prepare and freeze
Pour into ice cube trays, open-freeze until firm, then tip into a polythene bag, remove the air, seal, label and return to the freezer.
STORAGE TIME: As long as you like!

Water melons
Don't freeze water melons: they lose their texture when thawed.

Waxed paper See **Greaseproof paper**

Westphalian ham See **Ham, raw, cured**

White kidney beans See **Beans, dried**

Whitecurrants See **Redcurrants**

Whiting
Check with your fishmonger that the fish has not been previously frozen. The flesh should be firm and white with a fresh smell. If whole, the eyes and gills should be bright.

To prepare
Clean whole fish, remove the head and tail and fillet. Cut fillets into portions, if necessary. Rinse with cold water and pat dry on kitchen paper (paper towels).

To freeze
Interleave fillets with polythene interleave sheets or clingfilm (plastic wrap), then pack in polythene bags, remove the air, seal, label and freeze.
STORAGE TIME: 3 months

To thaw and serve
Thaw at room temperature for 2 hours, separating the fillets as soon as possible, then cook in your usual way, or cook from frozen, allowing 3–5 minutes' extra cooking time.

Whiting, smoked
Smoked whiting fillets are often called golden cutlets. Select bright-coloured fish with moist, but not wet, flesh. Avoid any that are drying at the thinner, tail end.

To prepare
Cut the fish into portion sizes, if necessary.

To freeze
Interleave with polythene interleave sheets or clingfilm (plastic wrap) and pack in polythene bags. Remove the air, seal, label and freeze.
STORAGE TIME: 3 months

To thaw and serve
Poach in milk or water from frozen, allowing 3–5 minutes' extra time.

Wine
Wine that has been opened will keep in a sealed container in a dark cupboard for a month or two but it can be frozen for longer. It can be used only for cooking, of course.

To freeze
Pour the wine dregs into ice cube trays. Freeze until firm. Tip in to a polythene bag, remove the air, seal, label and return to the freezer.
STORAGE TIME: 12 months

To thaw and serve
Add frozen cubes to any cooked dish for flavour.

Witch

Check with your fishmonger that the fish has not been previously frozen. The flesh should be firm with a fresh smell. The eyes should be bright.

To prepare
Rinse with cold water and pat dry on kitchen paper (paper towels).

To freeze
Interleave with polythene interleave sheets or clingfilm (plastic wrap), then pack in polythene bags, remove the air, seal, label and freeze.
STORAGE TIME: 3 months

To thaw and serve
Trim the fins and tails. Cook from frozen, in your usual way, allowing 5 minutes' extra cooking time, or thaw at room temperature for 2 hours first.

Woodcock

Allow one bird per person. Choose plump birds.

To prepare
They are usually sold undrawn. Clean them before freezing and put the heart, gizzard and liver in a small polythene bag to freeze separately from the bird. Rinse inside and out with cold water and pat dry on kitchen paper (paper towels). Truss.

To freeze
Protect the bone ends with foil, then pack in a polythene bag with the bag of giblets. Remove the air, seal, label and freeze.
STORAGE TIME: Birds 6 months, giblets 3 months

To thaw and serve
Thaw in the fridge for up to 24 hours and cook as soon as defrosted.

y

Yams

To prepare
Peel and cut into dice or even-sized pieces. Blanch for 2 minutes in boiling water with 15 ml/1 tbsp lemon juice added. Drain and plunge immediately in a bowl of iced water to cool. Drain and dry on kitchen paper (paper towels).

To freeze
Pack in convenient quantities in polythene bags. Remove the air, seal, label and freeze.
STORAGE TIME: 12 months

To thaw and serve
Dice: Boil in lightly salted water for about 8 minutes until tender, then mash or toss in butter.
Larger pieces: Thaw at room temperature until you can separate them, then toss in hot oil and roast for about 1 hour at the top of a preheated oven at 200°C/400°F/gas mark 6 (fan oven 180°C) until golden and tender.

Yeast
Fresh yeast freezes well – a boon if you prefer it to the dried varieties. Buy from a good baker, so you know it is very fresh.

To prepare and freeze
Cut into 15 g/½ oz pieces. Wrap in clingfilm (plastic wrap), then place in a rigid container. Remove the air, seal, label and freeze.
STORAGE TIME: 12 months

To thaw and use
Thaw at room temperature for about 30 minutes, or grate while still frozen, then thaw (this takes only 5–10 minutes). Use according to your recipes.

Yellow beans   See **Beans, yellow**

Yoghurt

Commercially sold yoghurts have stabiliser added so that they can be frozen but home-made yoghurt separates on thawing.

Yoghurts to be frozen must be very fresh. Don't freeze when nearly past their use-by date. If you freeze a large carton, it will need to be used within three days of thawing.

To freeze
Leave in their unopened original containers. Label and freeze.
STORAGE TIME: 1 month

To thaw and serve
Ideally, thaw overnight in the fridge (especially if defrosting a large carton). If necessary, thaw at room temperature but eat as soon as possible.

Yorkshire puddings

Yorkshire puddings freeze beautifully. You can, of course buy ready-made, but home-cooked are best!

To prepare
Make in your usual way. Cool once cooked.

To freeze
Pack in polythene bags. Remove the air, seal, label and freeze.
STORAGE TIME: 6 months

To thaw and serve
Reheat from frozen in a preheated oven at 200°C/400°F/gas mark 6 (fan oven 180°C) for about 5 minutes until crisp and hot through. They may be grilled (broiled), turning frequently, until crisp and hot, but take care as they burn easily. Don't reheat in the microwave because they will go soggy.

Z

Zabaglione

Zabaglione loses its volume on freezing. You can use whole eggs that have been frozen to make it, but make sure they are thawed completely before use.

Zucchini *See* **Courgettes**

index